"I've been a teacher for 20 years, and I work hard to stay good at it. Part of our success as educators is our willingness to learn more, to work smarter, and to continuously improve. In *Teach, Reflect, Learn,* Hall and Simeral have captured the essence of this drive: it's about how we think about our work! **Simple, fun to read, and useful, the options in here put the quest for excellence within reach.** Bring on the next 20 years!"

—Yasameen Sharif, former Science Teacher of the Year for Norfolk County and Brookline (MA) public school teacher

"For most of us, one of the biggest bumps we face on the road to personal improvement is being comfortable with conscious incompetence—becoming a novice all over again with better methods and avoiding sliding back into comfortable, yet inferior routines. Pete Hall and Alisa Simeral understand that teachers' professional growth isn't a simple technical—do-this, do-that—affair. Instead, it's deeply personal and often a bit scary. With research-based insights, compassion for teachers, humor, and practical examples, ***Teach, Reflect, Learn*** **provides a road map for teachers' journey to success,** helping them past the bumps they'll inevitably experience along the way and empowering teachers to, as they write, 'always strive to be a better you.'"

—Bryan Goodwin, president & CEO, McREL International, author of *Simply Better* and *The 12 Touchstones of Good Teaching*

"**A captivating teacher resource** that inspired me to use self-reflection in becoming more effective in the classroom. Pete and Alisa are passionate educators who motivate educators to change their thinking in their approach to building success in the classroom. **A refreshing must read!**"

—Tracy Titus, gifted resource teacher, Colorado Springs, CO

"Pete and Alisa's unique approach of emphasizing the reflection process and use of non-judgmental methods in making professional growth make me feel like they are genuinely interested and invested in me as an educator and person. The predictable chapter structure makes it a smooth read and simple to implement. **This real life guide is appropriate for any teacher or educator regardless of grade level, degree, experience, or subject area.** It provides useful tools, assessments, and surveys that can easily be translated into practice. I am very anxious to begin implementation. Why didn't I think of this?"

—Derek Cordell, principal, Pleasant Valley (NV) Elementary School

"Having been a teacher for twenty-two years, I sat down to read *Teach, Reflect, Learn* with a bit of a skeptical eye. After all, what was I going to learn from these authors that I hadn't already figured out during my tenure as an educator? It did not take me long to realize how wrong I was. I have always considered myself to be a reflective teacher, but through this book Mr. Hall and Ms. Simeral have given me specific tools to be reflective using targeted and explicit methods. I appreciated the anecdotes which helped to illustrate the effectiveness of these strategies in interesting and engaging ways. The self-assessment tool was especially powerful in helping me to look more closely at my instruction. It was eye-opening to realize how much of the continuum is still out in front of me! **This book not only addresses theoretical concepts, but provides ideas and information that I can put to use immediately** in order to become a more reflective, and thus more effective, teacher. I look forward to delving into my '6-week challenge' and striving to be a better me."

—Steve Staebell, teacher, Spokane (WA) Public Schools

"Teachers, consider this compelling question: *How reflective are you?* Then turn to this book as a viable resource, filled with dozens of tools, methods and strategies that foster your self-reflective tendencies. **This genius, yet at the same time very practical, must-read book** is the exact vehicle that can empower teachers to delve deeply into refining and perfecting the precision of their craft."

—Tina McIntyre, administrator (school improvement, accountability, and compliance), Region One (TX) Educational Service Center

"We understand our students' chances for success are heavily impacted by our own abilities as teachers. Striving to grow and improve, we continuously reflect on our work. We owe it to ourselves and to our students to employ a strategic and effective method of self-reflection to drive our growth as teachers. Enter Hall and Simeral's *Teach, Reflect, Learn.* **Packed with insights, strategies, and tools,** this book guides and informs our self-reflection, helps us to recognize and improve our reflective tendencies, and leads us to more deliberate and intentional instruction. Launch this endeavor on your own, with your colleagues, with your coach, or partnering with your administrator to begin refining your craft today!"

—Brad Kuntz, teacher, Gladstone (OR) High School and 2011 Outstanding Young Educator Award winner

"**This book is spot on.** The practical tools are exactly what teachers need to become reflective practitioners. We discuss the difference of assessment 'for' learning versus assessment 'of' learning and it is a hard concept for some to grasp. Consider the difference between reflection 'of' teaching versus reflection 'for' teaching. Reflective conversations have the power to transform teaching and learning."

—Lisa Garcia, superintendent, Point Isabel (TX) School District

"As a classroom teacher, I am always looking for ways to improve my craft. **In *Teach, Reflect, Learn*, I have found the ultimate DIY guide to continuous growth.** I have had the good fortune of working with both Pete and Alisa, and I can honestly say this: they not only practice what they preach, they also make it clear, straightforward, and easily integrated into the array of work we're already doing. For teachers, this is an amazing resource—a gift. I applaud my colleagues for picking it up and reading it—and taking action."

—Lisa Ramburado, teacher, Washoe County (NV) School District

"**What a motivational book!** *Teach, Reflect, Learn* has led me down a path to look inward, rather than outward to increase my capacity as an educator. There's incredible value in the act of self-reflection and this process has empowered me in great ways!"

—Mandi VanDellen, implementation specialist, Reno, NV

"**This book provides the necessary research-based reflective practice strategies for any teacher at any point in his or her profession.** The framework, tools, questions, and strategies provided in this text will help educators not only be reflective about their planning and instruction, but will also assist teachers on how to be reflective 'in the moment' of instruction, providing tools that will help pivot instruction immediately to meet the needs of all learners. No matter where you are in your teaching career the tools and strategies presented in this text are meant for you."

—Ignacio Lopez, vice provost for academic programs, National Louis University, Chicago, IL

Teach
Reflect
Learn

ASCD MEMBER BOOK

Many ASCD members received this book as a
member benefit upon its initial release.

Learn more at: **www.ascd.org/memberbooks**

Teach Reflect Learn

Building Your Capacity
for Success in the Classroom

PETE **HALL**

ALISA **SIMERAL**

Alexandria, Virginia USA

ASCD®

1703 N. Beauregard St. • Alexandria, VA 22311-1714 USA
Phone: 800-933-2723 or 703-578-9600 • Fax: 703-575-5400
Website: www.ascd.org • E-mail: member@ascd.org
Author guidelines: www.ascd.org/write

Judy Seltz, *Executive Director,* Stefani Roth, *Publisher;* Genny Ostertag, *Director, Content Acquisitions;* Julie Houtz, *Director, Book Editing & Production;* Jamie Greene, *Editor;* Thomas Lytle, *Graphic Designer;* Mike Kalyan, *Manager, Production Services;* Keith Demmons, *Senior Production Designer;* Andrea Wilson, *Senior Production Specialist*

All web links in this book are correct as of the publication date below but may have become inactive or otherwise modified since that time. If you notice a deactivated or changed link, please e-mail books@ascd.org with the words "Link Update" in the subject line. In your message, please specify the web link, the book title, and the page number on which the link appears.

PAPERBACK ISBN: 978-1-4166-2010-5   ASCD product #115040
PDF E-BOOK ISBN: 978-1-4166-2012-9; see Books in Print for other formats.

Quantity discounts: 10–49, 10%; 50+, 15%; 1,000+, special discounts (e-mail programteam@ascd.org or call 800-933-2723, ext. 5773, or 703-575-5773). For desk copies, go to www.ascd.org/deskcopy.

ASCD Member Book No. F15-6A (Apr. 2015 PSI+). ASCD Member Books mail to Premium (P), Select (S), and Institutional Plus (I+) members on this schedule: Jan, PSI+; Feb, P; Apr, PSI+; May, P; Jul, PSI+; Aug, P; Sep, PSI+; Nov, PSI+; Dec, P. For current details on membership, see www.ascd.org/membership.

Library of Congress Cataloging-in-Publication Data

Hall, Peter A., 1971-
  Teach, reflect, learn : building your capacity for success in the classroom / Pete Hall, Alisa Simeral.
    pages cm
  Includes bibliographical references and index.
    ISBN 978-1-4166-2010-5 (pbk. : alk. paper) 1. Reflective teaching. 2. Effective teaching. 3. Teaching—Evaluation. I. Title.
  LB1025.3.H345 2015
  371.102—dc23

                    2015000508

23 22 21 20 19 18 17 16 15   1 2 3 4 5 6 7 8 9 10 11 12

Teach, Reflect, Learn

Building Your Capacity for Success in the Classroom

Preface

"Building your capacity for success." That's quite a phrase, and it packs a significant wallop—in education and in life. We chose this title because we believe in the expansiveness of our individual and collective capacity. We view capacity not as a static measurement—say, how much capacity one's heart has for blood—but as a dynamic element of improvement, or how much capacity one's heart has for love (to continue the metaphor). Our capacity for success, like our capacity for love, knowledge, skill, excellence, learning, and growth, is limitless. And as we increase that capacity, we simultaneously increase our ability to affect the children with whom we work in positive ways.

Such was the case at Anderson Elementary School in Reno, Nevada, the site where we (the authors—Pete Hall and Alisa Simeral) first met and collaborated on a massive school turnaround project. In 2002, Anderson Elementary (with its diverse population, including 90 percent in poverty, 70 percent transient, and 60 percent ESL) was the only Title I school in Nevada to have failed to make its Adequate Yearly Progress goals for four consecutive years. Facing sanctions under the newly minted No Child Left Behind law, the school was bussing students to neighboring schools, carried a "Needs Improvement" label, was working with a state-directed school improvement team, and was assigned a brand-new principal. As Pete took the keys to the building, he was told quite plainly, "Good luck."

During the next two years, the staff and leadership team at Anderson made monumental changes, both structural and philosophical. Between adding a second 90-minute literacy block and launching collaboration that began the metamorphosis into a Professional Learning Community (PLC), the school began to take on a whole new appearance. More detail, for those inclined to read about the changes, can be found in the *Educational Leadership* article "A School Reclaims Itself" (Hall, 2005).

The initial results were staggering. What was once, statistically, the lowest-scoring school in the state had raised its student achievement rates significantly, earning recognition as Nevada's only high-poverty school to receive a "High Achieving" designation. Nevertheless, the staff and leadership at Anderson knew that these gains, though exciting and impactful, were short-lived. They needed refinement. They needed enduring change. They needed to build their individual and collective capacity for success.

Hiring Alisa as part of a vibrant and energetic team of three instructional coaches proved to be one of the most important moves the team made. From that point on, the staff at Anderson focused on developing their collective capacity through the tenets of the PLC and tended to the development of individuals' capacity through coaching and an emphasis on self-reflection.

As the gains continued and the staff grew—both closer together and forward toward excellence—we knew that we had stumbled upon something extraordinary. We continued to research the ideas surrounding self-reflective growth, its importance in contributing to professional effectiveness, and our ability to cultivate and develop it.

That's what led us to write *Building Teachers' Capacity for Success: A Collaborative Approach for Coaches and School Leaders* (Hall & Simeral, 2008). In its first iteration, the Continuum of Self-Reflection, one of the tools you'll read about in this book, was designed primarily for use by instructional coaches and administrators. Conceived as a tool to help support the reflective growth of teachers, the continuum provided coaching strategies and structures for providing feedback that could guide teachers toward their professional goals.

Schools and districts across the country soon embraced the continuum, adopted its practices, and worked diligently to engage in rigorous capacity-building practices. In many districts, our work has become the model for instructional coaching and has spurred many principals into providing tailored feedback to teachers through a systematic process of walkthroughs and reflective thought. The response and reception we've received from *Building Teachers' Capacity for Success* has been humbling and overwhelming, yet there has been an element missing.

One of our frustrations is that although it was certainly not our intent, the strategies included in *Building Teachers' Capacity for Success* are sometimes construed as something that's done *to* teachers. They are really supposed to be done *with* teachers. This book, then, is intended to be something *for* teachers! The approaches outlined in the following pages represent something that's done *together*, with teachers taking the reins of their own professional growth.

In the preface to our previous book, we very honestly wrote, "What follows are the current results of our investigations. We write *current* because as education evolves, information expands, and experience accrues, our understandings of the work we do will continue to change and evolve as well" (Hall & Simeral, 2008, p. x).

Now, we very honestly write: What follows are the current results of our investigations. We write *current* because as education evolves, information expands, and experience accrues, our understandings of the work we do will continue to change and evolve as well. A decade of experience putting this into practice in our own schools—in addition to our continued fervent research and the hundreds (or thousands) of schools that have adopted this model—has led us to this place: right here, right now.

We introduce Chapter 1 with an overview of the impact of teachers. This is foundational to our work, since it's critical for every teacher to see himself or herself as a viable contributor to the education of our youth. In fact, as you read, you'll see that we concur with the overwhelming research base that the teacher is (i.e., you are) the #1 determinant of student success.

An investigation of the idea and importance of self-reflection is the subject of Chapter 2. Since the majority of our work and the primary tools (the Continuum of Self-Reflection and the Reflective Cycle) are based on the development of one's self-reflective tendencies and skills, it makes sense to see how self-reflection fits into the bigger picture of teacher effectiveness and teacher evaluation systems. It's also important to understand how you, as the reader and practitioner, can take ownership of your own self-reflective development.

In Chapter 3, we provide a short self-assessment to gauge your current self-reflective tendencies. This will provide you with a launching point for the rigorous—and unbelievably rewarding—work that lies ahead. You'll take a brief quiz and analyze your results to help you determine where and how this work begins.

We leap into Chapter 4 with considerable enthusiasm as we share the Continuum of Self-Reflection: a gradient that will help you better understand your reflective tendencies. Here you will learn about the four stages that compose the continuum—unaware, conscious, action, and refinement—and you'll learn how the defining characteristics of each contribute to your overall reflective state of mind. From there, we share the vehicle that propels us forward through each stage—the Reflective Cycle—which is a process that reflective practitioners engage in regularly in order to deepen their reflective habits and hone their skills.

In Chapters 5–8, we describe each stage of the Continuum of Self-Reflection in greater detail, using the Reflective Cycle as our catalyst. Designed to provide a thorough description of the characteristics of our patterns of thought, each chapter presents a goal and road map for developing your own self-reflective tendencies, accuracy, and behaviors. Each of these chapters also provides a list of strategies and approaches for undertaking the work: by yourself, by focusing on your students, with colleagues, alongside an instructional coach, and in partnership with an administrator.

You'll head to a specific chapter based on the results of your self-assessment (in Chapter 3), not unlike the "choose your own adventure" books we read as kids. Chapter 5 covers the Unaware stage, Chapter 6 focuses on the Conscious stage, Chapter 7 highlights the Action stage, and Chapter 8 centers on the Refinement stage. Feel free to read all of the chapters to gain an overview of the entire continuum, though you'll get the greatest yield by focusing on the specific chapter that covers the stage in which you're currently operating as a reflective practitioner.

We wrap up with an anecdote in Chapter 9. Using an amalgam of the many wonderful teachers with whom we've worked, we share the story of Michele—a teacher who yearns to have a greater impact on the students she teaches. This narrative should help bring the Reflective Cycle and the stages of the Continuum of Self-Reflection to life and make continuous growth—and educational excellence—a viable possibility for every teacher who has the courage to embrace the challenge.

Sprinkled throughout the book, you'll encounter sidebars we've each written in first-person singular. Dubbed "Pete's Perspective" and "Alisa's Approach," these anecdotes, insights, and outlooks are designed to offer you a bit more detail, a tale from the trenches, or at least a glimpse into our personal experiences with the content. If successful, these additions will help offer flavor and zest to the text. Our hope is to connect with each reader on a personal and authentic level. We are, after all, traveling this path with you!

Now go get 'em!

Acknowledgments

We are forever grateful to the schools and districts (many of which we trained ourselves) that approach this work with tenacity and optimism. Thank you for carrying our work forward and continuing to put it into place. You're making a difference for kids, and we're refining our work because of your incredible efforts.

Also, we'd like to offer a shout-out to the legions of educators we've worked alongside, observed, listened to, copied, emulated, and learned from over the years. Thank you! On behalf of the students whose lives you've impacted, thank you even more! You're the inspiration for this work, and we owe you immeasurable gratitude.

Thank you to the good people at ASCD whose technical and practical input have breathed life into this project. To Genny Ostertag, whose unyielding faith that we could somehow transform our ideas into something somewhat readable, and to Jamie Greene, whose relentless fine-toothed comb has added clarity and precision, and to the behind-the-scenes team who created a presentable product in which we have much pride, we offer our thanks.

Last but not least, we share our eternal gratitude to our families—spouses, kids, pets, and others—who put up with us as we spent countless hours hogging the family computers and tapping away at the keyboards long into the evening. This is a labor of love, and without your love and support it just wouldn't be possible. We believe the result is worthwhile.

If You Can Read This, Thank a Teacher

To determine whether or not you need to continue reading, we'll begin this book with a short quiz. If you answer *yes* to any of the following questions, please put this book down, pour yourself a glass of chardonnay, and enjoy the beach. If not, then this book is for you.

Question 1
Are our students learning as much as they possibly can?   YES   NO

Question 2
Are our schools as effective as they can possibly be?   YES   NO

Question 3
Are my students achieving as much as they possibly can?   YES   NO

Question 4
Am I as effective as I can possibly be?   YES   NO

Teachers, administrators, lawmakers, politicians, parents, students, groundskeepers, auto mechanics, chefs, professional baseball players, and all other heretofore unnamed living humans agree: our schools could be better. Our students could learn more. Our teachers could teach more effectively. Our student achievement rates could be higher. Our achievement gaps could be closed. Not only *could* all these things occur, but they *can*. It's possible. It's likely. And—gasp!—it's not really that difficult.

We could inundate you with data about international test scores in reading and math right now, sharing the turbulent history of American education and the major events that led us to our current status, and we'd be sure to sigh in exasperation alongside you at the collective shortcomings of our nation. In fact, in our 2008 leadership text, *Building Teachers' Capacity for Success*, that's exactly how we built our case. That's actually part of the formula for school-improvement texts. Pick up any book on school leadership, best practices, or school improvement, and you'll read the same outline.

We trust that you're already living this reality. Our kids are not learning at the rates they could be learning, and, frankly, it's our responsibility as professional educators to improve the way we practice education in order to achieve that simple goal. So let's get moving, shall we? How do we improve our schools, our teaching, and our students' learning?

We build our capacity for success.

The Center of the Universe

It was a typical spring afternoon at an elementary school in Reno, Nevada. As the final bell rang, signifying the end of another school day, children cascaded out of the 2nd grade classroom—an exuberant cacophony of sing-song, delight, and energy. The teacher, having escorted her students to the bus lines and their awaiting parents, now sat wearily at her desk, exhausted by the demands of the day and the prospect of grading, lesson planning, and preparing for the following day's lessons.

The pitter-patter of gentle footsteps revealed the presence of a single returning youngster. With a toothless grin, the student dug into his backpack and pulled out a folded, handmade card. He extended it across the cluttered but organized desk, where his teacher warmly accepted it, their eyes meeting briefly. As she unfolded the card and read the handwritten inscription, her heart warmed.

"Teacher, you are the center of the universe."

In an instant, the teacher melted. The demands of the school's accountability system, the pace of the curriculum, the pressure to raise academic scores, the long hours and meager pay, and the sheer exhaustion she felt moments ago dissipated in the words of that simple card. With tears welling in her eyes, she looked up to thank her admirer for taking the time to share his gratitude. And as is so often the case in education, he was already gone.

With all due respect to this loving and appreciative 2nd grader's gesture, we'd like to bring the message a little closer to home and craft an astronomically correct metaphor to illustrate his point. We believe the teacher is—*you are*—the center of the solar system.

Whereas the universe is vast and infinite, our solar system has definable boundaries and very clear, understandable properties. The center of the solar system is our sun, which has remarkable similarities to each and every one of you. What does the sun do? It provides life, offers warmth, gives us light (one might even say it illuminates), allows us to shine, and helps us grow. Earth revolves around it, staying connected by an invisible relationship that is unyielding, resilient, and designed to strengthen the quality of life for all of the planet's inhabitants.

The sun is brilliant, consistent, strong, intense, abundant, and supportive. The sun is, indeed, a star. And so are you. For every child, every class, every course, every school, every district, and every setting, you are the center of the solar system. And this book is for you.

How Important is The Teacher?

Less than half a century ago, conventional wisdom did not hold that a teacher's influence could have much of an impact on an individual student's growth, much less on the academic gains of the masses. The influential Coleman Report reported that outside influences—namely, poverty and family upbringing—were better predictors of student success than anything else. In fact, it substantiated the ideas that a teacher was at the mercy of a child's social condition (Coleman, 1966). Seventeen years later, the U.S. National Commission on Excellence in Education (1983) published its damning report A Nation at Risk. Its thesis was clear: our education system was in shambles, we were falling behind our international competition, and our schools were the primary culprits.

These two ideas could not peacefully coexist. One claimed that teachers didn't matter; the other asserted that teachers were the cause of our collective struggles. But how could our schools be failing so considerably if the teachers inside them were at the mercy of poverty and parenting?

Then we had research on teacher quality.

John Hattie's 2009 meta-analysis, *Visible Learning,* painted a very clear picture of the factors influencing student achievement. By compiling hundreds of research studies spanning 30 years and involving millions of students, Hattie provides the preeminent foundation of research-supported "best practices." And guess what was at the top of the list? Teacher quality.

In fact, Hattie's study determined that 9 of the top 13 influences on student achievement were teacher- or teaching-related. The magnitude of this research project, along with the descriptions and commentary on the strategies therein, provide compelling reasons to renew a sense of optimism about our collective (and individual) ability to change the educational for-tunes of the students seated in front of us every day.

Other education researchers have weighed in to support these findings. When best-practices guru Robert Marzano penned *The Art and Science of Teaching* (2007), he dispelled any lingering doubts that teachers impact learning: "One can conclude that the question as to whether effective teachers make a significant difference in student achievement has been answered. They do!" (p. 2). Shortly thereafter, Marzano collaborated with Rick DuFour and offered this premise for school improvement: "Schools must utilize strategies that result in more good teaching in more class-rooms more of the time" (DuFour & Marzano, 2011, p. 20). Bryan Goodwin and Elizabeth Ross Hubbell of McREL International solidified this argu-ment by stating emphatically, "Decades of research suggest that effective teachers can have a tremendous, positive effect on student success" (2013, p. xiii).

Recently, the tide has turned again. Legislators, government officials, the media, and the public have reduced teaching to formulaic instruction, standardized tests, and a simplified emphasis on scores. In an age where data drive all that we do, it's easy to forget that education is ultimately a people-centered business. Teachers are human, and that's a good thing. Even the push for online learning, virtual classes, and a computer for every child relies heavily on the fact that there's a person behind it all. Robots, even those with advanced artificial intelligence capabilities, cannot repli-cate a teacher's ability to build relationships, create dynamic learning expe-riences, provide differentiated feedback, and spur students' love of learning.

We can have automated teller machines dispense money from our bank accounts, but we can't have automated teaching machines. We need teachers.

Alisa's Approach

I'll never forget the day Mrs. Johnson walked into my office. She hesi-tantly asked if she could speak with me and closed the door behind her.

Sitting down, she burst into tears. "I just need to cry for a moment and then I'll be okay. My class is so low this year. They have so many needs. Alexis and her family just got kicked out of their house and are living out of a motel. My new student, Kai, refuses to do any work—he's a very angry child. Both of his parents are in jail, and he just was taken out of foster care to live with his grandma. I have two non-English speakers, three students on daily behavior plans, and eight that are receiving academic interventions right now—several of whom I have major concerns about. My heart is breaking for this class and I'm overwhelmed."

This scenario is all too familiar for anyone who has spent time inside a school. Far beyond curriculum, standards, and test scores are the daily challenges of teaching children who come to school with a limitless supply of problems and struggles. We teach because we want children to grow, learn, and become successful adults, but there's so much more to the story.

We dry tears. We break up fights, mediate conflicts, and mentor others through tough social situations. We work to keep sleep-deprived students alert and engaged. We hug students who have experienced the emotional trauma of their parents' separation, divorce, or abandonment. We comfort students who experience a death in the family, drug overdose, neighborhood shooting, or physical or sexual abuse. We purchase clothing, backpacks, school supplies, food, and books so students have one less thing to worry about.

Teachers are on the front lines each and every day. They absorb the joys and pains of every child who walks through the classroom door.

Mrs. Johnson rallied and walked out of my office that day. She walked back into her classroom and proceeded to do exactly what she has always done. She cared for, loved, and supported each of her students. She sought out new strategies, tried old ones, and figured out a way to help every child learn. And her students? They thrived and grew, engaged and learned. They left that classroom at the end of the year better individuals because of the investment Mrs. Johnson made in their lives.

Put Your Money Where Your Teacher Is

How important is the teacher? There are historical ties to their reverence. To wit: the famous Greek philosopher Aristotle extolled the virtues of the educator by stating, "Those who educate children well are more to be honored than they who produce them; for these only gave them life, those the art of living well." And that was in 325 BCE, just a few years before No Child Left Behind!

Let's consider the purpose of schooling: to educate the masses and prepare individuals for successful participation in society. Horace Mann, education reformer of the early 19th century, helped to define the original calling by stating, "Education then, beyond all other devices of human origin, is the great equalizer of the conditions of men, the balance-wheel of the social machinery." How can we measure an individual's success as a citizen? One way is to examine the bottom line.

Recently, two major studies have examined the collective and individual financial impact of having high-quality teachers. In one landmark project, researchers Raj Chetty and John Friedman of Harvard University and Jonah Rockoff of Columbia University examined the long-range earnings potential of students who were assigned to teachers with high value-added rankings (i.e., those whose impact on a single group of students was significantly higher than their peers', according to various assessment measures). Keep in mind that this study was published by the National Bureau of Economic Research, so it carries quite a bit of clout (Chetty, Friedman, & Rockoff, 2011).

With a statistical process free of bias and a case size of 2.5 million students, the results are staggering. Having a high-quality teacher, even for one year, can have a tremendous impact across many measures. Students assigned to high value–added teachers are more likely to attend college, earn higher salaries, and save more for retirement. They are also less likely to become teenage parents. These are all desirable outcomes for an education system working for the betterment of society, wouldn't you agree?

For the number-crunchers out there, this study revealed an average increase of $80,000 in lifetime earnings for just one year of schooling with a high value–added teacher. Do the math: 13 years in the K–12 system with exceptional teachers could have an impact of $1.24 million in additional earnings for one student! For a high value–added teacher with 25 students, that's an economic gain of $2 million per year for just one class.

A second study, conducted by economic analyst Eric Hanushek (2011) of Stanford University, also examined the collective financial impact of increasing teacher quality. While he identified the impact of high value–added teachers on individual earnings potential, he simultaneously proposed a more widespread economic rationale for improving the teaching force. According to his calculations, there exists an immense benefit to cultivating teacher quality. Over the course of a lifetime, increasing our teachers' value could yield the U.S. economy an additional $112 trillion.

What's a great teacher worth? Plenty.

Hero: A New Definition

Recently, a teacher was spotted in a crowded middle school hallway in Spokane, Washington, sporting a T-shirt emblazoned with this message: "I'm a teacher. What's your superpower?"

This got us thinking. In our society, where do teachers rank? Publicly, financially, socially, and popularly, how do our educators fare? Wouldn't it be nice if this were the storybook narrative passed along, from generation to generation?

The cries were faint but audible. Locked in a high tower in a dangerous castle guarded by a terrible dragon, the helpless maiden longed for a hero in shining armor to rescue her.

Alas, the tower was constructed of trauma and poverty, a life pieced together by the day, the hour, the minute, and housed in the chaotic reality of struggle: the struggle to learn, the struggle to connect, and the struggle to survive. The castle, perhaps decrepit or maybe just overlooked, was encircled by a dangerous moat of uncertainty and fading hope. The dragon, relentless and hissing, feasted on ambition and drank the tears of despair while guarding its innocent but vulnerable captive.

Ho! What glorious knight arrived at breakneck pace across the moonlit plain? 'Twas the teacher, of course, riding a stallion of courage, carrying a shield of empathy, and waving a sword of steel expectations. Across the moat in a single bound, our hero provided a safe and caring environment for our young innocent to learn, persevere, excel, and overcome.

Once extracted, our youngster tamed the dragon, rebuilt the castle, and remodeled the tower into an observatory . . . so she could keep a good eye on the entire kingdom. The teacher saved the day!

There are plenty of examples of heroic teachers, individuals with seemingly superhuman amounts of gusto, insight, perseverance, and interpersonal skills . . . and versions of them indeed exist in Hollywood. We know the stories of Erin Gruwell (*The Freedom Writers Diary*), Jaime Escalante (*Stand and Deliver*), and Lou Anne Johnson (*Dangerous Minds*) because of the films in which they were portrayed.

However, those stories are few and far between. It is our contention that within every teacher is a hero. One needn't leap onto desktops to motivate learners (though Robin Williams's excellent performance in *Dead Poets Society* might inspire us to do just that!). True teaching heroism, in our humble opinion, is found in the day-to-day grind. It's in the way that teachers lead their students down the circuitous path to learning, navigating rough terrain and all sorts of obstacles, creatively and passionately insisting that success is the only option.

Teachers are our everyday heroes, thanks to their resolve, grit, energy, commitment, kindness, benevolence, honor, endurance, wisdom . . . this list could reach to the stars (or at least the sun).

Pete's Perspective

When I was a child growing up in Oregon, my 6th grade language arts teacher was Mrs. Andrews. There's one thing I want to make perfectly clear right up front: Mrs. Andrews was a great teacher. And when I say great, I mean she was wonderful. Fantastic. The best.

You might ask what it was that made Mrs. Andrews such a great teacher. Well, there were a lot of things. I'm sure she had a solid grasp on the curriculum. She must have known a lot about formative assessments. She was a thorough lesson-plan writer. And she must have worked collaboratively with her colleagues in the building. Most likely, she had all of the characteristics you might read about in a research article about "effective teachers."

But that wasn't what made her great to me.

To me, you see, Mrs. Andrews wasn't just a teacher. She was an angel. When I walked into her classroom every day, I felt like the king of the world. Each day, I held on tight to my chair, for fear that I might actually start flying around the room. When the bell rang and class began, I was drawn into her lesson like a tractor beam. I participated, became engaged, and was engrossed.

Mrs. Andrews made me feel special. She asked about my day, what I was up to, and when my next basketball game was. I was pretty sure that every time she smiled, it was for me. She was attentive to my work and always asked questions about the content that made me think harder and pay more attention, which I did gladly. She demanded excellence from me and never settled for less. She had high expectations, and you'd better believe I was going to meet them! Her classroom was safe, inviting, warm, and fun. Again, I was certain that she set it up that way just for me. To her, obviously, I was special.

A certain amount of time has passed since I was in 6th grade, and I've now been working in schools as a teacher or administrator for the past 15 years. As I reflect on my memories and thoughts of Mrs. Andrews, a new realization has hit me. Mrs. Andrews made me feel special, sure, and that's terrific. But what truly made her a great teacher was something else: she made *everybody* feel special. She welcomed every child into her classroom, enthusiastically building relationships and embracing the challenge of teaching every student in the most effective way possible. She raised the bar for all of us. That was her calling, and she relished it.

I can't recall all of the material I learned in that 6th grade class, but I'm quite certain I used that knowledge and those skills to succeed in high school, college, and beyond. After all these years, what sticks with me even more is the difference one teacher made in my life—the self-confidence, desire to learn more, high expectations I began to place on myself, and joy.

Every so often, I think of that fabulous, magnificent teacher. I then think of the hundreds (maybe thousands) of students who likely felt just as I did in her class: like the most special person in the world, someone truly capable of doing anything I set my mind to.

Then I think of the thousands upon thousands of teachers just like her, dedicating everything they've got to the children under their care—making them feel special, inspiring them, encouraging them, and teaching them.

To each and every teacher out there, today I share this refrain: Thank you, Mrs. Andrews. Thank you.

If our interpretation of the overwhelming research on teacher quality is indeed accurate, then it's our collective responsibility to engage in an ongoing pursuit of excellence. Let's make *continuous improvement* the new status quo. As we become more effective, our students learn more and our yield becomes more robust and bountiful. We cannot wait. Just think of the impact we can have on student learning, on the development of our youth, on the quality of our schools, and on the state of affairs in the profession of education. Just think . . . reflect . . . that's the key.

For most of us, education isn't just a job or profession or something we do during the school year. It's a calling. And we're not called to mediocrity. We're called to make a difference. To impact the future. To change students' lives. To help our young people become the amazing, wonderful human beings they're meant to be.

And our charge—to maximize our impact through continuous improvement—is a calling we must heed. Let's spread our professional wings, grow as reflective practitioners and skilled educators, and fulfill the destiny of that calling.

2

Reflections on Self-Reflection

"It is the language of reflection that deepens our knowledge of who we are in relation to others in a community of learners."
—Carole Miller & Juliana Saxton, University of Victoria

Let's assume that you trust the research, your years of experience, and that unrelenting feeling in your gut that tells you teachers truly matter. And since yielding high levels of student learning is our ultimate goal, our collective charge right now is to improve our professional practice and increase our positive impact on academic achievement. This is neither new nor easy. So how do we accomplish these lofty goals? We speak the "language of reflection." We engage in rigorous, ongoing self-reflection about our professional responsibilities.

Self-Reflection: Growth That Endures

Think for a moment about something at which you'd consider yourself to be very good, maybe even an expert. If you're like the rest of us, you've developed this expertise over time; you weren't always good at it. So how did you develop this skill? What were some of the behaviors you employed? How did you learn new and different strategies to refine your capabilities? As you grew in proficiency, what changed? How did these changes arise?

Growth, improvement, progress, and development don't just happen overnight, and they typically don't happen accidentally. They're a result of intentionality, planning, conscious effort, and thought. You had to think about it—a lot, probably—to get good at it. So let's just cut to the chase, shall we? Sink your gray matter into the following questions:

- How did your thinking about this skill evolve?
- When did you first consciously think about your current skill level and your desire to improve?
- Did you construct an intentional plan to engage in betterment strategies?
- How did that plan change over time, as you experienced setbacks and accomplishments along the way?
- Were you aware of your improvement as your skills increased?
- How often did you dedicate your brain power to this growth?

The particular skill or area of expertise you considered for this exercise isn't important. You might have thought about skiing, crocheting, fishing, trimming rose bushes, or calligraphy. Why isn't it significant? Because, in the words of John Dewey, "It's not the doing that matters; it's the thinking about the doing" (quoted in Archambault, 1974, p. 321). The ability to self-reflect is based in your brain—not in any specific content, skill, strategy, or approach. Self-reflection is context-independent.

To paraphrase Mr. Dewey, we might offer this: Doing the right things matters; self-reflection matters more.

A Definition of Self-Reflection

What do we mean, precisely, when we use the term self-reflection? Our working definition includes an overarching concept (i.e., the act of exerting mental energy about our professional responsibilities) and a series of very specific reflective behaviors:

- Gaining awareness of our educational surroundings (students, content, and pedagogy).

- Planning deliberately and taking action with intentionality.

- Assessing the impact of our decisions and actions.

- Adjusting our course of action based on the feedback we receive from those assessments.

- Engaging in this reflective cycle continuously.

Expertise does not come naturally. Developing a skill takes time, effort, energy, and a hefty dose of self-reflection. The difference between learning a skill and being able to implement it effectively resides in our capacity to engage in deep, continuous, rigorous thought about that skill. Technical expertise is one thing; practical expertise is another thing altogether.

Pete's Perspective

In high school, I was a model student in my Spanish classes. I could conjugate verbs, recall tricky vocabulary words, and string together complex sentences with the best of them. When it was time to write an essay about my trip to the shopping mall, I got high marks. During my 10-minute oral presentation to the class, I rocked the house. And then, my freshman year in college, I had a one-on-one conversation assessment in Spanish 101, and the rug was pulled out from under me.

What happened? My technical expertise was exceptional. My ability to apply that skill, however, lacked significantly. Why? Because I was focused on completing tasks without attending to the bigger picture of why I was learning the language in the first place—to assist in communication.

Fortunately, I had the opportunity to travel to Honduras with my father and brother soon after that disastrous chat with my professor. Once immersed in the language and culture, I noticed that my proficiency increased. Because neither my father nor my brother spoke any

Spanish, my ability to communicate with guides, waiters, hotel operators, and everyone else we encountered was truly the difference between a fun trip and a horrible family catastrophe.

To help us along, I immersed myself in an updated study of the language—through a new, more urgent lens—during our visit. I directed all of my mental energy toward understanding and communicating clearly. I contemplated what words I'd need to use to accomplish certain tasks, I attended to the accents of local residents, and I listened for key terms. In short, I wrapped my head around the practical skill of communication and insisted on my own success. My success—as measured by our successful and enjoyable trip through that beautiful country—was later explained by my good friend and colleague Andre Wicks: "There's nothing more powerful than a made-up mind."

The Doing-Thinking Gap

You may be aware of the knowing-doing gap, which was first popularized in the influential book *The Knowing-Doing Gap: How Smart Companies Turn Knowledge into Action* (Pfeffer & Sutton, 2000). That book describes the chasm between what we know we should do and what we actually do—and how we might bridge that rift. Later, we'll discuss this in greater detail. In the meantime, there's another, lesser-known gap we'd like to address: the doing-thinking gap.

Many of us, either in our personal or professional lives (or both), fall into habits and routines for how we go about our business. Often, we just do things the way we do because, well, that's the way we do it. We don't really think about why we do it that way; we just do. The doing-thinking gap exists for that precise reason—we don't think about the doing. A colleague of ours shared a story that might help illustrate this phenomenon. You may have heard it before.

As the story goes, a man spent a nice evening with his wife and in-laws. As his mother-in-law prepared lamb for their dinner, she lopped off the shank and threw it in the trash before placing the tray in the oven. The man noticed this peculiar action but said nothing.

A few months later, his wife was preparing lamb for a dinner party they were hosting. Just as her mother had done, she cut off the shank before placing the lamb in the oven. This time, the man asked, "Why did you cut off the shank?"

"I don't really know," she replied. "My mom always did that, and she learned from her mother, who always did that. I guess that's a family secret that somehow makes the lamb taste even better. That's just the way we do it in our family." Unconvinced, the man enjoyed his dinner.

It was at his wife's grandparents' 50th wedding anniversary the following summer that he finally obtained the answer he sought. Sitting next to her grandmother, the man asked, "This may be a silly question, but why do you cut off the shank before cooking lamb in the oven?" His grandmother-in-law smiled and responded, "Son, when I was a young lady first learning how to cook, we had a tiny oven. The lamb wouldn't fit if I left the shank attached, so I had to cut it off in order to cook it."

In education, we are just as susceptible to this rascally doing-thinking gap. A little more than a decade ago, when *Classroom Instruction That Works* (Marzano, Pickering, & Pollock, 2001)—perhaps the most popular and recognized meta-analysis of teaching—arrived in our mailboxes, we were drawn to the "research-based" authority and strategies provided by McREL and Bob Marzano. Many educators, in their haste and zeal to do right by their kids and improve their practice, embraced this text as a must-do checklist.

At the top of that list, of course, was the first strategy detailed in the book: Identifying Similarities and Differences. What followed was a legion of teachers creating a flurry of lessons based on the Venn diagram, whether it was an appropriate educational tool for the particular learning target or not. In educators' minds, the assumption of a universal connection between this strategy and student learning was enough justification to employ the approach.

We just did the strategy; we didn't think about it. Though this is a rather comical example, it portrays the unintended consequences of the doing-thinking gap. Marzano himself has since clarified the research, explaining that just doing these nine strategies isn't sufficient; teachers must do them well in order to impact student learning positively. And that takes thought.

You Hold the Reins

Is it possible to develop self-reflective skills? Yes. Are there ways to improve self-reflective accuracy? Absolutely. Can we build our self-reflective tendencies? Definitely. Are highly effective, reflective teachers born or made? The latter. You're in charge of your own self-reflective development, and we're here to help you learn how to do it.

In *Drive: The Surprising Truth about What Motivates Us* (2009), Daniel Pink discusses a new way of looking at motivation. Rather than acquiescing to extrinsic forces (e.g., carrots and sticks), we are innately compelled to increase our performance due to intrinsic factors. The three elements that most significantly contribute to our self-propelled quest for excellence are autonomy, mastery, and purpose.

The idea of autonomy forms a particularly relevant bond with self-reflection, as both speak to the idea of an internal locus of control. You are in charge of your own thinking. You don't need to wait for someone else to arrive and tell you what to do, how to do it, what to think about it, and why it's important. With self-reflection, you can—and you must—take the reins of your own growth, development, and improvement.

With so many professional responsibilities determined for us in education (such as rigid daily bell schedules, a fixed calendar, adopted curricula, Common Core State Standards, prescribed lessons, and preordained professional development plans), it is essential to our continued growth—not to mention our sanity—to have some semblance of ownership over our own development. We must take an active role in learning new information; applying new approaches; and accessing instructional coaches, administrators, peers, Professional Learning Community members, and other resources. To a considerable degree, our professional growth rests in our own hands.

It is a common human characteristic to seek mastery in whatever we do. If we are going to spend time, energy, and resources on something, then we'd like to be good at it. Makes sense, right? As we discussed earlier, in order to increase skill and cultivate expertise at anything, we've got to engage in rigorous and consistent reflection about it. This certainly applies to all aspects of teaching, from planning to data analysis and, most assuredly, to the delivery of high-quality classroom instruction.

Pink (2009) describes one of the more exciting elements of mastery by describing it as a mind-set. If we believe that we can grow and improve, then we're much more likely to accomplish our goals. Stanford University psychologist Carol Dweck (2006) offered a liberating view of a "growth mind-set," in which we're better served when we're oriented toward a learning goal (e.g., learning strategies to better address the needs of individual learners) rather than a performance goal (e.g., increasing the percentage of proficient students on a unit assessment). Both contribute to the overarching idea that by working harder, smarter, and more thoughtfully and by truly becoming engaged in the growth process, we can build our capacity for success—as both reflective practitioners and instructional deliverers.

Interestingly, one of the simplest and most direct ways to eradicate the doing-thinking gap is by identifying and pursuing a specific purpose for engaging in work. Simon Sinek (2011), a professional thinker, business trainer, and optimist, explains the necessary connection between our purpose and our work. When there exists an ineradicable link between the two, our productivity soars and our sense of fulfillment goes through the roof.

Educators, as a whole, tend to make this connection naturally. Education is often seen as a calling—a profession that attracts people who yearn to make a difference in the world. We are enthralled by the idea that our daily work will better the lives of the young people under our charge, we are inspired to impact the future positively, and we are stirred to influence the greater good. This is bigger than just being a good teacher and making academic gains on performance assessments. This is about changing the world for the better—one student, one class, one day, and one school at a time. What better motivation is there? What nobler calling can you imagine? And if this is indeed your passion, your mission, or your raison d'être, then aren't you likewise committed to continuous growth and professional improvement?

Alisa's Approach

The musings below capture a snapshot of my ongoing reflections around sugar.

- I really like sugar.
- I know too much sugar is bad for me.
- It's very difficult to pass up snack-size Butterfinger bars, especially the ones sitting in the staff lounge bowl.
- What's this? The average American consumes 22 teaspoons of sugar daily? And proposed sugar guidelines tell us to have no more than 6 teaspoons a day?
- I wonder how much sugar I eat each day. Perhaps I should start keeping track.
- Wow! I need to cut back. I'm going sugar-free for a week.
- I'm not eating sugar today. Not eating sugar. I'm not eating sugar. No sugar.
- This is hard.
- Really. Hard.
- I'll just have one. They're tiny . . .
- Yesterday was not a good day.
- Starting fresh. Maybe if I carry around something healthy.
- I made it through a day. Yippee!
- Planning snacks in advance definitely helps.

- It's been a week already? I think I can go one more!
- I know too much sugar is bad for me.
- I really like sugar.

Self-Reflection and Teacher Evaluation Systems

For the uninitiated, the idea of developing one's self-reflection is rather nebulous. It might appear to be a vague concept with tenuous connections to teaching performance. Teachers face immense pressure (both within the education system and in the greater public) to demonstrate accountability for their performance. The public wants results, and a renewed emphasis on high-stakes teacher evaluation systems adds a daunting element to the profession. So how does this fit in?

Interestingly, almost every teacher-evaluation model we surveyed includes some element of self-reflection. Each of the two most popular instructional frameworks, Bob Marzano's *The Art and Science of Teaching* (2007) and Charlotte Danielson's *Enhancing Professional Practice* (2007), includes specific domains allocated for reflecting on teaching. Others mention self-reflection in one form or another, dotting the landscape with a peripheral emphasis on the idea that intentional thought contributes to effective teaching. But why?

As we've already mentioned, in order to be good at anything, you need to be thoughtful, intentional, and reflective about your practice. Self-reflection is context-independent. It is a transferrable skill, meaning it's part of the arsenal you can carry in your scabbard to wield at whatever crosses your path, regardless of content, curricula, standards, teaching methodologies, or grade level. It is the lynchpin, the key cog, the critical link. Self-reflection can bridge the doing-thinking gap, knowing-doing gap, and any other gap that might otherwise impede your progress. Developing these abilities will enable you to master whatever skills, strategies, approaches, or methods you set your mind to.

Reflection also fits nicely into any technical skill, such as planning, classroom management, instructional delivery, data analysis, collaboration, ongoing professional growth, response to administrative feedback, work with instructional coaches, and parent relationships. Regardless of the teaching framework in use in your school or district, the ability to consider the technical aspects of instruction thoughtfully offers you a wide base upon which to build your expertise. In short, developing self-reflective skills and tendencies will better prepare you to succeed in any evaluation system. As frameworks change and are updated, as standards are refined, as curricula and materials are adopted, as administrators come and go, and as the education pendulum swings back and forth, you'll be equipped for success.

National Boards: Reflection and Effectiveness

The highest level of professional certification available in the United States—offered by the National Board for Professional Teaching Standards—is obtained by teachers who can successfully demonstrate their impact on student learning. To do this, they must submit videos, work samples, and detailed reflective essays that analyze their work and influence. In fact, the National Board Certification process relies heavily on a teacher's self-reflective tendencies and accuracy. Proposition #4 (of the Five Core Propositions upon which Board Certification is based) reads as follows:

> Teachers think systematically about their practice and learn from experience.
>
> - NBCTs [National Board Certified Teachers] model what it means to be an educated person—they read, they question, they create, and they are willing to try new things.
> - They are familiar with learning theories and instructional strategies and stay abreast of current issues in American education.
> - They critically examine their practice on a regular basis to deepen knowledge, expand their repertoire of skills, and

incorporate new findings into their practice. (National Board for Professional Teaching Standards, 2002)

Though we aren't necessarily advocating that you pursue National Board Certification, it's certainly a worthwhile goal and a widely recognized acknowledgment of teaching excellence. And as you develop your self-reflective skills through the processes and methods outlined in this book, you'll be well on your way to tackling the requirements for submitting the reflective essays in your application! In the meantime, let's engage in some introspection: What will it take to grow as a reflective practitioner?

An Investment That Pays

Developing reflective skills, accuracy, and tendencies is clearly a very worthwhile ambition. And, as is the case with most worthy pursuits, it will require you to dedicate yourself wholly to the process. Growth in your ability to think, reason, consider, weigh, ponder, assess, deliberate, reflect, and act on that reflection takes time, energy, and commitment. This involves working collaboratively with peers, administrators, mentors, and coaches. It won't always be easy. This isn't a "read-it-and-now-I'm-good" sort of endeavor. As you dive into this process of reflection and growth, we ask that you do so intentionally, wholeheartedly, and optimistically.

Prepare yourself for the rigors of thought. It requires time—perhaps solitude—so you can fully connect with your thinking. When we take the time to process and plan, we feel more in control, more productive, and more successful. Our brains need the space that is created when we refine our thinking. With the challenge of making hundreds, if not thousands, of decisions every day, how we filter the input cascading at us is essential to our well-being. Trying to fill a water bottle from a fire hydrant will result in spills and frustration. We tend to live in overflow mode, which causes us to seek strategies that help us survive rather than thrive. Engaging in regular reflection allows us to dial the spigot down, regulate the input, and once again take control over our thoughts and actions.

If you're ready, buckle up. Making the commitment is the first step, and we commend you on your willingness to embark on the journey. The second step is to take stock of your current reflective tendencies and abilities. In the following chapter, we'll help you do just that.

How reflective are you right now?

Reflective Self-Assessment Tool

"Knowing others is intelligence; knowing yourself is true wisdom.
Mastering others is strength; mastering yourself is true power."

—Lao Tzu

In order to gauge how (and how accurately, how deeply, and how often) you engage in self-reflection, we have created a short self-assessment tool. At its conclusion, you'll analyze your responses and compute a simple score. This score, while certainly not static or definitive, will offer you information about your self-reflective abilities by identifying the stage on the Continuum of Self-Reflection at which you currently reflect and operate. The Continuum of Self-Reflection and its four stages are described in more detail in Chapter 4. Chapters 5–8 are dedicated to offering you dozens of strategies for building your self-reflective tendencies that are matched to your current stage.

So how reflective are you right now? Let's find out.

Directions for Using the Self-Assessment

Before you get started, it's important to emphasize this advice: Be honest. Choose the statement that resonates with you first. There are no right or wrong answers nor are there good or bad scores—there are only choices that match your patterns of thinking and information that informs your next steps. You could probably read the scenarios and pretty easily choose the options that indicate stronger reflective tendencies, but if that's not an honest appraisal of your thinking, then you'll get erroneous feedback that will send you down the wrong path. This tool is for *your* use, so again: Be honest.

Read each of the following 10 scenarios and circle the letter next to the response that is most accurate, most likely to be true, or most often the approach you would take in the given situation. You will likely find that some of the scenarios have more than one option that matches your style. In that case, go with your gut—what would you typically do? After the final scenario, you'll record your responses on a scoring chart and follow the next set of directions to analyze the results.

Here you go:

1. When planning for today's (or tomorrow's) lesson, I . . .

    A. Begin with the content and activities that we will be covering and occasionally prepare specific teaching strategies.

    B. Utilize recent student assessment data to determine what I'm going to teach and how I'm going to teach it.

    C. Spend most of my time deciding which instructional methods I'll use to meet the specific needs of my students, relying on unit plans to determine the content.

    D. Consult the teacher's edition of the textbook and follow the lessons provided.

2. When considering how often I reflect on my teaching, I . . .

    A. Routinely reflect after teaching a lesson and/or analyzing an assessment.

    B. Reflect after grading student work or when prompted by an administrator, coach, or colleague.

    C. Occasionally reflect after grading assignments or quizzes.

    D. Continuously reflect, including during the lesson itself.

3. When planning to address student misconceptions, I . . .

    A. Address them when they occur, because it is difficult to tell where students will struggle.

    B. Follow the established plan for the lesson from beginning to end.

    C. Analyze student work to determine what struggles students are having and then plan to address them.

    D. Plan for check-ins throughout the lesson, so I can provide support as necessary.

4. When I encounter students who struggle in a lesson, I . . .

    A. Analyze each student's specific struggles to determine a course of action designed to address them.

    B. Can't always tell why they struggle, because there are so many variables.

    C. Realize I have little control over how some students perform, so I continue to encourage them.

    D. Look at my teaching strategies to see if changing them might have a better effect.

5. When attempting to reengage students who are off-task, I . . .

    A. Stop the lesson, regroup students, and resume the lesson when I'm ready.

    B. Address the situation with a variety of preplanned engagement strategies.

    C. Employ a strategy that I am most comfortable with and have used before with success.

    D. Use ideas from the lesson plan I'm following and/or power through in hopes that students will reengage.

6. When I ask questions in class, I . . .

    A. Ask questions that I have prepared in advance.

    B. Ask questions from a collection I have prepared, varying my asking/answering strategies.

    C. Ask questions that come to me while I'm teaching and that will continue to move the lesson forward.

    D. Ask questions that are included (as written) in the lesson plan.

7. When describing the students I teach each day, I . . .

    A. Can identify those who are most/least successful, who struggle with assignments, and who are the first to finish.

    B. Can identify individual academic profiles and can cite the latest assessment data.

    C. Tend to focus on their personalities, behavioral patterns, and overarching descriptive traits.

    D. Can explain the latest assessment data, including anecdotal information, and can describe how they are grouped for instruction.

8. When students are struggling in a lesson, I . . .

    A. Stick with the lesson plan to make sure we cover the required material.

    B. Attempt to address the learning gaps by modifying the following day's lesson.

    C. Adjust my instructional approaches immediately.

D. Go back and reteach the problems they got wrong.

9. When determining the level of success in a particular unit, I . . .

A. Monitor the progress of individual students through continuous formative and summative assessment strategies.

B. Monitor class performance on lesson assignments and/or quizzes to see if students are "getting it."

C. Monitor performance by administering an end-of-unit test and noting student scores.

D. Monitor class progress through formative and summative assessment strategies.

10. When reflecting on my students' assessment performance levels, I . . .

A. Check the grade book to see how the students fared.

B. Can describe individual students and the specific concepts they have mastered.

C. Explain with detail how groups of students performed.

D. Provide information about how the class did as a whole.

Self-Assessment Scoring Guide

Now that you have honestly and accurately completed the self-assessment, it's time to collect some data about your reflective practices. Record your responses in Figure 3.1. Write the score you received in the far-right column for each question.

The sum of these 10 scores is your total score, which notes the stage on the Continuum of Self-Reflection that most likely characterizes your self-reflective tendencies. Mark that score on the Self-Assessment Scoring

Scale in Figure 3.2 and use the following guide to determine where you currently operate along the continuum:

- 10–14 points: Unaware Stage
- 15–24 points: Conscious Stage
- 25–34 points: Action Stage
- 35–40 points: Refinement Stage

FIGURE 3.1

Self-Assessment Scoring Chart

Question	A	B	C	D	Your Score
1	2	3	4	1	
2	3	1	2	4	
3	2	1	4	3	
4	4	1	2	3	
5	2	4	3	1	
6	3	4	2	1	
7	2	3	1	4	
8	1	3	4	2	
9	4	2	1	3	
10	1	4	3	2	
TOTAL	*(Add your question scores to determine your overall score.)*				

FIGURE 3.2
Self-Assessment Scoring Scale

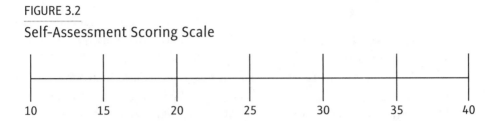

Wherever you scored, wonderful! You may want to be somewhere else, you may be working to get somewhere else, or you may be on your way to somewhere else. In the meantime, though, you're right where you are—reminiscent of the scene in the movie *Austin Powers: International Man of Mystery* when our hero points to an unsuspecting gentleman and exclaims, "There you are!"

The man looks quizzically at the secret agent and asks, "Do I know you?"

Austin replies, "No, but that's where you are, right there!"

With that encouragement, let's wrap our minds around what you're going to do with this information.

Pete's Perspective

I often find myself reminding teachers that there is no good or bad score with this self-assessment. There is no "better than" or "worse than" here. This tool provides us with some information about how we think. Self-reflection is a skill, a habit of mind, and a behavior that we can strengthen, hone, refine, and grow. Wherever you are, and whatever you scored, and however you engage in thinking about the work you do, you're about to begin the process—composed almost entirely of a succession of baby steps—of moving forward along the Continuum of Self-Reflection.

Have you ever taken a personality quiz or a learning profile assessment? Have you ever measured your multiple intelligences or determined your strengths in an assessment tool? Do you know what "color" you are? We all have areas in which we're strong, skilled, and talented. That's what makes us special! Thankfully, we can build on those strengths and improve our personal and professional lives.

Think about Michael Jordan, arguably the greatest basketball player who ever lived. Some might argue that his excellence was based on the fact that he was graced with exceptional physical skills and athletic talent. That's true, but he also had an incredible will to win. He practiced as hard as he played. He enjoyed the competition and thrived on growth. Early in his career, he could score and dunk, but his team didn't win. It wasn't until he became the league's top defender, developed a deadly jump shot, and learned to play with his teammates that his team won six championships. This took dedication, hard work, and focus—focused thought, focused (and intentional) decision making, focused adjustments, and focused reflection. Growth is within all of us.

It's essential for educators to take the reins of their own professional learning. You're motivated and committed to do so, and you see the connection between building your self-reflective skills and enhancing your instructional impact. Now that you've taken a preliminary self-assessment to gauge your reflective tendencies, it's time to saddle up, grab those reins firmly, and begin the work of building your own capacity.

What are you going to do with the results of this assessment?

Alisa's Approach

As I've shared this tool with teachers, one common theme keeps popping up. They find the questions prompt more reflection than anything else! The teachers who field-tested this assessment craved the opportunity to go through their responses with someone, to digest and reflect on the data, and to discuss how their thinking affects their doing.

So . . . talk about it with someone! Take the assessment with a colleague, an instructional coach, your mentor, an administrator, or a trusted friend. Share your responses, explain your thinking, and exchange feedback. Since there are no "right" or "wrong" answers and we have suspended value judgments, the conversation is what's important. The reflections matter most. You'll find that as you expand the discussion to a team, a department, or an entire staff of teachers, the richness of the dialogue expands exponentially. You needn't keep this to yourself; go ahead and share.

In Chapter 4, we'll explain the Continuum of Self-Reflection, provide some details about each of the four stages (Unaware, Conscious, Action, and Refinement), and introduce you to the reflective cycle that guides the process. As you read and reflect on your own thinking, you will begin preparing for the challenges—the incredibly rewarding and deeply meaningful challenges—that lie ahead.

Feet in the stirrups? Let's ride.

The Continuum of Self-Reflection

....

"Thinking is the hardest work there is, which is probably the reason so few engage in it."

—Henry Ford

We're big fans of metaphors, especially when we learn something new and can relate it to something familiar. Our favorite metaphor for describing the Continuum of Self-Reflection has to do with a relatively unknown but effective manner of losing weight. In workshops, we begin by asking our audience this question: Are you aware that there is a direct connection between toothpaste and weight loss? Almost universally, we are met with quizzical looks, so we proceed to explain our point.

Consider this. Before today, you've been living your life just like normal. Blissfully unaware of a strategy you could use to make your life happier and healthier and to contribute to some weight loss, you march forth as you always have. Perhaps you believe you're making healthy choices, maybe you lament some aspect of your physical well-being, or maybe you don't even think about health that much. In any case, you're firmly in the Unaware stage on the Continuum of Self-Reflection.

Over the past few years, multiple research studies have been published in medical journals explaining the surprising link between toothpaste and weight loss. Evidently, brushing your teeth immediately after each meal suppresses your urge to snack between meals, and the sweetness of minty toothpaste halts the cravings for those desserts you might otherwise gravitate toward, further reducing your daily caloric intake. Additionally, the act of brushing your teeth sends a message to your brain that you've finished eating, so your body can begin its work of metabolizing the food.

So, armed with this information, you might consider brushing your teeth a little more frequently. Your morning routine is already solid, and you begin to brush your teeth immediately after dinner, rather than waiting until right before bed. Brushing your teeth after lunch at school is still a challenge, though, because you've got a million things going on and, hey, you're a teacher. You've barely got time to eat at school, let alone brush your teeth afterward! Despite your best intentions, your application of this healthy practice is inconsistent. You know about this strategy, but you aren't making the intentional decision to enact it consistently. Your actions now place you in the Conscious stage on the Continuum of Self-Reflection.

A couple of months down the road, you find yourself at the doctor's office during your annual physical exam. After conducting the routine battery of tests with needles and probes, your doctor frowns and says, "I'm a little concerned about your physical health. You're carrying around a couple of extra pounds, your blood pressure is slightly elevated, and I'm not sure if you're aware of this, but you're in a very high-stress profession! Something's got to change."

After some reflection, you remember the information about toothbrushing and weight loss, and you decide to give this thing a shot. With newfound motivation, you start a toothbrushing regimen that would make Mr. Colgate jealous. You purchase a slew of pocket toothbrushes and keep them in your desk, your bag, and your car and scattered around your house. You're brushing every chance you get, and it seems to be working. Your mind is completely wrapped around this idea. In just a few weeks, you've lost a couple of pounds, your blood pressure has dropped, your endurance is up, and you're feeling pretty good. Because you've turned knowledge into consistent action that has proven results, you've now stepped into the Action stage on the Continuum of Self-Reflection.

Now, if a relatively simple strategy like brushing your teeth more intentionally can have such a significant effect, imagine what other healthy habits could do! You pick up a book on healthy eating at the bookstore and begin to explore several diet plans. Over time, you learn a lot and can pick and choose healthy strategies that work best for you, your lifestyle, and your goals. This sophisticated level of thinking is defined as the Refinement stage on the Continuum of Self-Reflection.

As Figure 4.1 demonstrates, the Continuum of Self-Reflection is composed of four stages: Unaware, Conscious, Action, and Refinement. To be very clear, these stages are really states of mind, levels of self-awareness, and phases in the self-reflective process that ultimately lead to you becoming a reflective practitioner. We've chosen the term stage to emphasize the point that self-reflection is a progressive process. We do not mean to suggest a categorical definition. In fact, an individual may demonstrate characteristics of more than one stage simultaneously and be in different stages while teaching different subjects or courses, for example.

FIGURE 4.1

Continuum of Self-Reflection

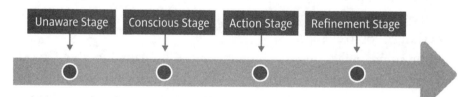

Our intent is for you to view the characteristics associated with each stage more as reference points than as a checklist of behaviors that need to be checked off before advancing to the next stage. In a nutshell, the Continuum of Self-Reflection is a tool that helps you identify how you think about the work you do. In order to get to where you want to go, you have to begin by knowing your current location.

Alisa's Approach

It started over a bottle of wine. Cabernet, if I remember correctly. Wendy and I were two of five new teachers hired at an elementary school that year, and we had become fast friends. One of the conditions of our employment was a requirement to complete a five-credit course, and we'd just turned in our final project. We met at her house after school to celebrate the culmination of many hours of hard work. Conversation turned to what parts of the learning we'd actually implement in our own classrooms and quickly led into a spirited discourse about the types of educators we wanted to become, the types of classrooms we wanted to foster, and the path we needed to take to get there.

It was Wendy's assertion that, while building our knowledge through coursework was fine and dandy, it was deliberate thinking—and our responses to that thinking—that would turn us into the remarkable teachers we sought to be.

Fast-forward nine years. I'd been hired as a site-based literacy coach with the simple charge to support teachers in the classroom wherever they needed me. Struggling with my job description and questioning my ability to have an impact outside of the classroom, I picked up the phone and dialed Wendy's number for a much-needed pep talk.

"Remember the night we solved the world's problems on my back porch over a bottle of wine?" she asked. "Remember the type of educators we swore we'd strive to be? At the end of the day, if you can get your teachers to think more deeply about what they do—What's working in their classrooms? What's not working? Why?—then you'll be successful. Developing our self-reflection habits is the path to our highest potential."

I quickly realized that as an instructional coach, I had access to dozens of teachers who reflected, in all sorts of different ways—with various degrees of depth, accuracy, and frequency. This was just the springboard I needed! Thus began my investigation into each of the stages of reflection and the different approaches we could take to increase our self-reflective tendencies.

The Continuum of Self-Reflection was born.

Certain questions now arise: How do I do this? How do I propel myself into a deeper stage of reflection? How do I become a reflective practitioner? This brings us to the heart of this book—the "meat and potatoes," if you will: the reflective cycle.

The Reflective Cycle

If you think of the stages along the Continuum of Self-Reflection as stops on a long and dusty highway, then the reflective cycle (see Figure 4.2) is the vehicle used to get you to your destination: becoming a reflective practitioner. As you'll see in the following chapters, the wheel sometimes starts slowly for folks in the Unaware stage. It may even get stuck a time or two as you pass through the Conscious stage. Eventually, though, it gathers traction and picks up speed as it rolls through the Action stage and heads into the Refinement stage, where the reflective practitioner operates.

Let's zoom in a little bit on the vehicle that propels us forward on this venture. We start by identifying four characteristics (or attributes, behaviors, or habits of mind) that combine to define effective, accurate reflection. These four components (identified in the inner sections of our wheel) are critical to clarifying how we think and how our thinking affects our professional performance.

All teachers demonstrate, to varying degrees, skills and tendencies related to each of five areas: Awareness of Instructional Reality, Intentionality of Actions, Ability to Accurately Assess, Capability to Adjust Actions, and Frequency of Reflection. These gradients of skill, habits, and reflective accuracy are illustrated on a sliding scale or continuum: the Continuum of Self-Reflection.

Interestingly, growth in self-reflective tendencies tends to follow a repeated (and repeatable) pattern. We have come to call this the Reflective Cycle. A teacher must necessarily develop awareness before seeking to act with intentionality, engage in intentional practice prior to assessing the impact of one's actions, and determine impact prior to enacting interventions.

FIGURE 4.2
The Reflective Cycle

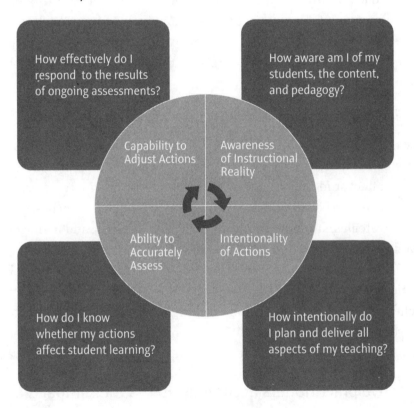

Reflective practitioners have awareness of their instructional realities.

How aware am I of my students, the content, and pedagogy? A teacher with awareness is knowledgeable about each and every student in his or her class, including his or her individual academic levels, interests, learning profiles, and instructional needs (Tomlinson, 2014). Having awareness means possessing a deep understanding of the content, including prerequisite relationships, connections across content and subject areas, and common misconceptions that will need to be addressed. Such a teacher knows how to facilitate learning in a manner that students understand; in other words, individual learning styles are connected to the right pedagogical approach in order to maximize retention. This is a practitioner who is acutely aware of every aspect of classroom instruction. Charlotte Danielson (2007) describes awareness as an attribute that allows a teacher to comprehensively "see" what's going on in the classroom, in the plan book, and in all measures of learning.

Reflective practitioners are intentional in their actions.

How intentionally do I plan and deliver all aspects of my teaching? The next step in the reflective cycle consists of a teacher taking intentional steps to affect student learning. With awareness of the instructional reality, a teacher can better select learning goals, curricula, materials, instructional strategies, student groupings, learning activities, and management strategies to meet the needs of specific students in the classroom. This is done, most assuredly, on purpose. Implementing research-based best practices is a solid strategy, though there is a big difference between a teacher who performs a specific teaching act and one who does it well. According to Hattie (2009), "What 'some' teachers do matters—especially those who teach in a most deliberate and visible manner" (p.22).

Reflective practitioners accurately assess their impact.

How do I know whether my actions affect student learning? Once a teacher engages in intentional, calculated actions, it is imperative to determine whether or not the specific actions resulted in the intended outcomes. Implementing some form of assessment is the next step in the reflective cycle. Assessment tools are varied and must be matched to the task and purpose: student observations, performance assessments, surveys, quizzes, and other methods of data collection inform the teacher of the degree to which Teaching Strategy A resulted in Student Learning B.

Reflective practitioners adjust their actions on-the-fly.

How effectively do I respond to the results of ongoing assessments? What a teacher does with assessment data often determines the outcome of a particular unit, lesson, or instructional strategy. In the reflective cycle, teachers armed with real-time assessment data can immediately adapt their approach, modify their lesson, or even stop and regroup. These decisions—based on ongoing, formative assessment information—help clarify misconceptions, address holes in learning, recalibrate energy, increase engagement, and provide an alternative method for helping students access their learning. Highly reflective teachers know that they have a powerful and immediate effect on student learning, and if students are struggling, then they can swiftly get them back on track by intervening in calculated and meaningful ways (Hattie, 2009).

Reflective practitioners engage in ongoing reflection.

How often do I reflect about my teaching and student learning? Reflection is a habit; as such, it must be developed. Engaging in the reflective cycle requires practice, diligence, and focus. Reflective practitioners have mastered this process and seem to engage in ongoing reflection almost intuitively. They do not wait for someone to pose a reflective prompt or to suggest that they attend to something. Rather, they are constantly alert to the reality of their classrooms, they make decisions intentionally, they assess the impact of those decisions, and they take immediate actions to course-correct as necessary.

How do I use this information?

You have your results from the self-assessment in Chapter 3, which offers you a pretty accurate on-ramp to the road toward deep self-reflection. You also have a solid understanding of the reflective cycle, so you're equipped to take your show on the road.

Our reflective tendencies are fluid. As we develop and strengthen our skills and habits, we flow along the Continuum of Self-Reflection—with an end goal of reaching the Refinement stage, which is characterized by constant thought and continuous reflection. There is no finish line, just movement toward a pattern of thinking that leads to more effective professional practice. It's an exciting pursuit and a noble endeavor, to say the least.

Pete's Perspective

Some years ago, I adopted a philosophy of life that is summarized in seven words: Always strive to be a better you. This simple phrase helps keep me calibrated at work, at home, and at play. Quite simply, I've embraced a mind-set that is aligned with the pursuit of continuous improvement. No matter what I do, and no matter how well I do it, I can always do it better.

Without going into too much detail, this philosophy is based on the ancient Greek principle of *paideia,* which held that our goal in life was to realize our full potential. However, our potential expands as we near it, leaving us with a never-ending quest for excellence—an eternal pursuit of growth. This helps me as I strive to write more clearly, use more humor, connect more with my wife and children, swear less on the golf course, reflect more deeply, or whatever it is that garners my attention.

It is in this spirit that we've engaged in this labor of love. This is why we've created the strengths-based, growth-oriented Continuum of Self-Reflection. And this is why we believe that if you step forward earnestly, you'll be rewarded with greater reflective habits, more effective classroom practice, and a richer career flowering with the growth and achievement of your students.

In the following four chapters, we'll go into depth and detail about each of the four stages of the Continuum of Self-Reflection. We'll outline the characteristics and goals for each stage, and we'll offer a wide selection of strategies—specific to each stage—meant to encourage deeper reflective habits. We neither expect nor insist that you complete (or even attempt) all of the strategies listed. Rather, we ask that you view them as options.

Select the approaches that you feel are within your Zone of Proximal Development (ZPD). The ZPD, as you'll recall from Vygostky (1978), is that special place where you are challenging yourself without overextending your abilities; you're stretching your capacity just enough to grow in a safe environment.

To engage in that learning, your responsibility is to read the chapter that corresponds to the stage at which you currently operate, according to the results of your self-assessment. Therefore, if you

- Scored 10–14, turn to Chapter 5: The Unaware Stage.

- Scored 15–24, turn to Chapter 6: The Conscious Stage.

- Scored 25–34, turn to Chapter 7: The Action Stage.

- Scored 35–40, turn to Chapter 8: The Refinement Stage.

After you've read the chapter appropriate for you, if you'd like to read about the other stages, then go for it. The more knowledge you acquire, the better you'll understand the entire process.

Remember, the Continuum of Self-Reflection is a tool. It is designed to guide and support your growth so you can develop your reflective skills. But please don't stop there. Heed the immortal words of Napoleon Bonaparte: "Take time to deliberate, but when the time for action comes, stop thinking and go in."

It's time for action, folks. Go on in.

The Unaware Stage: What Does *Unaware* Mean, Anyway?

*"I learned that courage was not the absence of fear, but the
triumph over it. The brave man is not he who does not feel
afraid, but he who conquers that fear."*

—Nelson Mandela

We've all been there, and most likely we didn't even know it. Take, for
example, the mysterious case of whole fat versus low fat when considering weight-loss strategies. Conventional wisdom and common sense have
directed us for years to stay away from whole fats and opt instead for low-
fat choices. If our goal is to lose weight, low-fat milk would be a better
option than whole-fat milk, for instance.

Or so we thought. In February 2014, National Public Radio (NPR) aired
the popular story "The Full-Fat Paradox" on stations across the country.
At its heart, the reporter debunked the myth that whole-fat dairy leads to
weight gain (Aubrey, 2014). Instead, she reported, new studies have shown
that high-fat dairy is associated with a lower risk for obesity. Whether it's
because whole-fat dairy makes us feel fuller more rapidly, or because of bioac-
tive matter in the milk that alters our metabolism, or because of the beneficial

omega-3 fatty acids, the result is clear: whole-fat dairy is more conducive to weight loss (Holmberg & Thelin, 2013; Kratz, Baars, & Guyenet, 2013).

If this information weren't staggering enough, try this on for size: These findings came on the heels of another NPR story, "Whole Milk or Skim: Study Links Fattier Milk to Slimmer Kids," in which—you guessed it—the author cited research that shows a positive correlation between skim milk and weight gain (Aubrey, 2013). So, after hearing for decades that fat is bad for us, new research is beginning to point us in another direction. Drinking whole milk, eating full-fat yogurt, using butter, and plopping a dollop of whipping cream on our strawberries is being touted as a healthier diet to pursue and might actually make us leaner!

If this is news to you, congratulate yourself! You've just become *aware* of a situation or fact you previously did not know. If you were skeptical of the findings and looked for confirmation in the research studies we cited, all the better. If this information compels you to further investigate your dietary options as you seek to become a healthier person, then you are clearly on the right track. Regardless of your experience or expertise following dietary guidelines and eating healthfully, you've unlearned, relearned, and expanded your knowledge in a way that can help you make healthier grocery lists from here on out.

In short, you've become aware of a better mousetrap, and you'd like to use it.

As educators, we can draw the same parallel to ourselves in the classroom. At some point or another, we all experience what it means to be "unaware" when it comes to understanding students, grasping content we're required to teach, knowing the best pedagogical strategy to implement in a given lesson, or identifying an intervention strategy that will work for a child who is not making progress. Regardless of how much experience you have, increased awareness will always lead to boosting your capacity as an educator.

FIGURE 5.1

The Unaware Stage

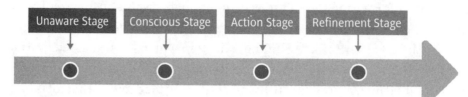

If the results of your self-assessment tool returned a score in the 10–14 range, that's an indication that you are currently operating in the Unaware stage, a term we use to describe teachers who have not yet learned about certain teaching strategies, aren't yet attuned to the finer details of their class and students, and do not yet reflect deeply about their particular responsibilities. As we build from this stage, teachers must become aware of the instructional realities of their classrooms.

We encourage you to remember that the Continuum of Self-Reflection is a tool we use to help us identify how we think. It gives us a direction for building our self-reflective tendencies and accuracy in a way that will enable us to become more effective decision makers and practitioners in the classroom. There is no value—no "better than" or "worse than"—assigned to any of the stages on the continuum; there are just terms that describe how we think about our work. So let's consider the term more closely.

unaware: *having no knowledge of a situation or a fact*

Alvin Toffler, author and former associate editor of *Fortune* magazine, shares this telling quote: "The illiterate of the 21st century will not be those who cannot read and write, but those who cannot learn, unlearn, and relearn" (Toffler, 1970). To be certain, he's not saying that reading and writing are unimportant; he's making the critical point that the most successful individuals today are those who have the ability to reflect—those who are aware of what they know, recognize that what they know is always subject to change, and have the ability to undo and relearn knowledge. Therefore, they are able to revise their belief systems.

Knowledge Is Power

That raises a few hairs on the back of your neck, doesn't it? Belief systems are subject to change, and it's possible for *your* belief system to change. Perhaps it was ingrained in us as children, or perhaps it was taught to us as adults, but the belief that admitting we don't know something is a sign of weakness or ineptitude is embedded deep within most of us. We feel that asking for help or changing a belief makes us look weak or needy. It's only through confronting this myth head-on that we recognize the opposite to be the case. Being unaware is not a sign of weakness; it's only a sign of weakness if you don't do something about it. The more you learn, the more insights you can build on top of the things you already know until one day you realize that the constant pursuit of knowledge is the basis of your professional success and personal fulfillment.

Does this mean we are encouraging you to ride every educational tide, movement, and fad that comes along in order to become more successful? Not at all. Education is famous for its pendulum swings that create a chorus of "This too shall pass" in the staff lounge. We're actually promoting the idea that you should learn as much as you can about every initiative so you can better evaluate the effectiveness of each. The more aware you are of the realities and nuances in your classroom—instructional, behavioral, curricular, or otherwise—the better equipped you'll be to make thoughtful, intentional decisions that best serve your students. In order to build awareness of these realities, we start with becoming introspective and building awareness of what we know and what we don't know.

Are you starting to wonder what it is that you don't know? This is just the beginning. You'll find that the more you reflect on what you know, the more you'll realize what you don't know. It can be a scary—yet extremely rewarding—process, and we commend you for taking the first step.

Knowledge is power only inasmuch as we use it. As German poet and writer Johann Wolfgang von Goethe advised, "It is not enough to have knowledge; one must also apply it. It is not enough to have wishes; one must also accomplish." It is in that spirit that we implore you to seek out new information and implement it in your professional practice.

Meet the Teachers

Consider the implications of this as we visit a couple of classrooms and take a closer look at two teachers who are in the Unaware stage.

Visit 1: Mrs. Damon (secondary): Mrs. Damon, a 24-year veteran teacher, is seated at the front of the classroom. As she graphs an algebraic equation on a coordinate plane under the document camera, the image is projected on the screen. She is showing the third problem in a set of problems from the class textbook.

The students, seated in rows facing the screen, are generally on task. Mrs. Damon kindly reminds the class, "You should be copying these graphs on your own worksheets as I model them, so you'll be able to complete today's assignment."

A slight commotion catches Mrs. Damon's attention, and she looks up. Two students are turned around, talking with a classmate. This is a frequent occurrence, and Mrs. Damon raises an eyebrow.

"Boys," she says. "Attention up here, please." The boys turn forward momentarily, but then resume their conversation when Mrs. Damon returns to the document camera.

Later, Mrs. Damon explains, "I worry about those boys. They don't seem to enjoy math or take school seriously at all. It's not really that hard for the kids to earn a good grade in my class—I always model the problems, and the textbook offers a very clear explanation. If they're failing my class, then they'll have a real eye-opener next year when they're in high school, that's for sure."

Visit 2: Mr. Barnett (elementary): It is unmistakable that Mr. Barnett is a popular teacher. Even though it's just a few months into his first year teaching 2nd grade, he has gained a favorable reputation as "the fun teacher." There isn't a bare spot on the wall, thanks to a peppering of student-created drawings between multiple San Antonio Spurs posters.

At present, the students are transitioning from centers (which included computer games, a puzzle, a sight-word activity, letter writing, and the library nook) and gathering on the carpet for a read-aloud. The children are in no particular hurry, and Mr. Barnett engages in some playful banter with two girls near the drinking fountain.

After several minutes, the majority of the class is on the carpet and Mr. Barnett asks, "Okay, so what book do we want to read today?" The students excitedly call out several titles. "Oh, so you want me to read *Finklehopper Frog* again?" He knew they would—they love the voices he makes.

When asked about his students' reading levels, Mr. Barnett smiles and shrugs. "I don't know the exact levels," he responds, "but they're all growing, I'm sure. I really enjoy this class, and I like teaching more than I thought I would. These kids are fantastic. At this point in their lives, it's my job to make sure they enjoy coming to school every day."

Characteristics of an Unaware-Stage Teacher

As you may have picked up from the descriptions of Mrs. Damon's and Mr. Barnett's classrooms, teachers in the Unaware stage have a few common characteristics. These two teachers, for example, demonstrate some telling indicators: they are comfortable in the way they do things, they are unaware of better alternatives, and they see no need to change. The way they think about the act of teaching directly impacts the way they carry out their job responsibilities.

Referring back to the reflective cycle, let's look a bit deeper at each of the five components of reflection through the lens of a teacher in the Unaware stage.

FIGURE 5.2

The Reflective Cycle

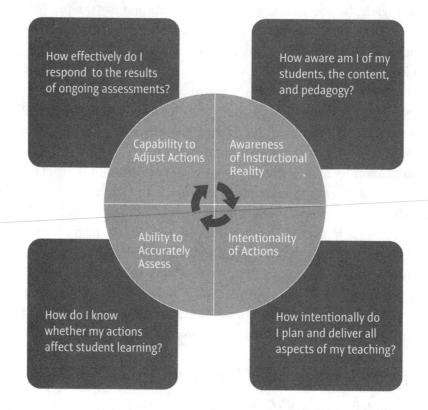

Awareness of Instructional Reality: How aware am I of my students, the content, and pedagogy? When asked to describe students in the classroom, teachers in the Unaware stage can typically identify the students who are behaviorally challenging, those who struggle to complete assignments, and those who are the first to finish tasks. Unaware-stage teachers can describe in global terms what they are teaching (within a subject area) and most often find confidence in presenting a lesson plan that has been prepared for them or that they have used before.

Intentionality of Actions: How intentionally do I plan and deliver all aspects of my teaching? Teachers in the Unaware stage rely heavily on the teacher's edition of the course textbook. Most often, their lessons follow a prescribed pattern: the teacher prepares materials, the teacher teaches the lesson, students participate in various activities, the teacher gives assignments as homework or practice, the students submit their work, the teacher grades and reports the scores, and the class proceeds to the next lesson. Unaware-stage teachers have a classwide set of rules, procedures, and expectations, and they address behavioral issues and learning within those guidelines.

Ability to Accurately Assess: How do I know whether my actions affect student learning? In the Unaware stage, an assessment or exam signals the end of a lesson or unit, and these tests are used to measure the amount of learning that has occurred. Teachers in the Unaware stage gauge the effectiveness of their lessons by measuring the amount of material covered, whether students were able to complete the tasks in the allotted time, and students' scores on graded assignments. Students receive feedback and information regarding their learning in the form of scores and grades on assignments, projects, tests, and final exams.

Capability to Adjust Actions: How effectively do I respond to the results of ongoing assessments? Often, teachers in the Unaware stage have very firmly established routines. These patterns of instruction allow them to usher the class through the required content at the necessary pace for completion within the established time frame. When students do not do well on an assessment or exam, the teacher may occasionally go back and reteach or review material. Because that touch-up is not part of the routine, the onus is on each student to change his or her work ethic, behavior, or attitude if he or she wants to learn. In other words, Unaware-stage teachers tend to follow a traditional pattern of teaching.

Frequency of Reflection: How often do I reflect? When they reflect, teachers in the Unaware stage usually do so after grading larger projects, assignments, and tests. With prompting from a colleague, an instructional coach, or an administrator, they may engage in some generic reflections on a more frequent basis. Unaware-stage teachers tend to reflect on student behaviors, project completion, class grade reports, and their personal feelings about their students' progress. They have yet to incorporate the reflective cycle (i.e., building awareness, taking intentional action, accurately assessing, and adjusting their work) into their regular routine.

Goal for the Unaware Stage

Remember: Knowledge is power! To this end, your goal in the Unaware stage should be to become more aware about yourself, your students, your content, your teaching methods, and your professional responsibilities. In essence, we want to reshape the way you look at your classroom, students, and teaching methods to become more aware of your instructional realities. As you grow in awareness, you will simultaneously develop your understanding of the distinct connection between your teaching behaviors and your students' achievement levels. And you'll want to learn more! Aristotle said it best: "The more you know, the more you know you don't know."

Growing Along the Continuum

To progress along the Continuum of Self-Reflection is to deepen your thoughtfulness about your professional practice. Having clear targets is a proven effective strategy for enhancing learning, so we've provided clear targets for each of the five key components of the reflective cycle. As you build your capacity as a reflective practitioner, and as you head toward the Conscious stage, we ask that you consider the following points.

Observe. The first step in gaining awareness is to pay attention to what's going on. On the surface, this sounds simple enough. However, the devil is in the details. You must be intentional about looking for, and noticing, different components of your classroom. To expand your generic observations about students in your class, look for trends and patterns. When do certain students struggle with behavior, attention, or work completion? In addition, attend to the details of the content you are teaching. How do different skills link together within a unit? When considering your instruction, identify the strategy (or strategies) that you gravitate toward. Then consider how the use of varied strategies might support deeper learning by more students.

Think Intentionally. The theme of intentionality weaves a thread through every aspect of self-reflective behaviors. As a reflective practitioner, you should leave nothing to chance! This means that your planning and preparation become ever more important. As you learn more about your students as learners, you can begin to create plans to address the differences among them—through intentional partnering, engagement strategies, and instructional techniques. An enormously important key for building intentionality into your repertoire is to write it down. All of it. Your learning targets, lesson plans, assessment strategy, management plan, engagement techniques, and rationale behind implementing each of them (if you'd really like to bolster your reflective habits) should all be a part of your written record.

Notice Learning. As you build intentionality and attention into your approach, the next component that will earn your focus is that of results. Are students learning what you're intending them to learn, and how do you know? The first step, which you've surely done, is to identify, clarify, and communicate the lesson or unit learning objective(s). Then, rather than wait until a project is finished or a test is graded, begin looking intentionally at students' work while they are working. Ask students to explain the learning target, describe the progress they're making, and share their own level of performance with you. Of course, you can also judge the quality of their work and the depth of their learning for yourself. By taking quick peeks at student work and using those as a formative assessment tool, you will have a quicker, more authentic, real-time gauge of your students' learning.

Make Changes. Once you have gathered some important information about your students' progress toward their learning objectives, you will most likely encounter some students who are struggling. Maybe many students are struggling. Fortunately, since you've uncovered these struggles in the midst of a lesson, an activity, or an assignment (as opposed to afterward), you're in an ideal position to make instructional adaptations to address these issues. This will be a challenging step for you; it requires a significant change in perspective. Simply covering the material is not sufficient; rather, ensuring high levels of learning for all students is the ultimate goal.

Practice Reflection. Becoming a reflective practitioner, as you have probably gathered, is not something that occurs by accident. Developing robust, consistent reflective routines involves quite a bit of intentionality and dedication. Becoming aware of the realities of your classroom, planning intentionally into all aspects of a lesson, assessing student learning and the effectiveness of your actions, and adjusting as necessary all require more frequent, deliberate reflection on your part. The more you think about what you've done (or what you're about to do), the more you're able to grow as a reflective teacher.

Alisa's Approach

I'd always aspired to be a "real" runner—the kind of person who can head out and knock off 10 miles before breakfast or who runs with her abs exposed, with her head held high, and with long, strong strides. (Yes, just like those beautiful Nike commercials.) So, two years ago, with this vision in my head, I decided to sign up for my first long-distance race. I pounded the pavement for miles in an attempt to prepare. However, after several weeks, I became increasingly frustrated. I wasn't getting stronger, wasn't running faster, and most certainly didn't feel like I was turning into the natural athlete I wanted to be.

It was during this training period that I met up with a runner friend. He'd competed on a sprint relay team in college and offered to give me some pointers. I jogged alongside him for about a mile before he honed in on my stance and began to suggest a few things. He specifically mentioned the need to tighten my core, stand straighter, and not lean forward. For the better part of an hour he demonstrated perfect posture and position. He tried to identify and explain the differences between how we ran. I struggled to copy what he showed me, feeling awkward and not understanding exactly what I was supposed to be doing. On our way home, we passed another runner. My friend was quick to draw attention to the specifics of her posture and all of a sudden, the light bulb went off. I was watching a reflection of myself. Her head was down, shoulders hunched forward, and her arms were crossing her body rather than swinging parallel to it. She needed to straighten up, push her shoulders back, and look ahead. I was able to finally grasp what my friend had been so patient in trying to explain. It was a defining moment!

I still can't emulate my friend's perfect stance, but I now see the sport in a completely different light. I notice all runners around me—how they place their feet, move their arms, lean forward, lean back, and hold their heads. For the first time, I can distinguish among styles. I see what I never noticed before. As my awareness grows, so does my capacity as an athlete.

Where Do I Start?

This is the exciting part, isn't it? You hold the reins. Growing in your reflective abilities, tendencies, and accuracy can be a daunting venture. As Brazilian educator Paulo Freire (whose theory of critical pedagogy is instrumental in our thinking) has said, "Reflection and action must never be undertaken independently" (Freire, 1970). So grab a pen and a pad, your favorite laptop or tablet, or whatever your tool of choice is to record your ideas and track your thoughts; the reflecting hour is upon us.

We've compiled a thorough collection of viable strategies designed to increase your reflective habits, including tackling your own self-directed learning, engaging in student-focused analysis, accessing your colleagues within a Professional Learning Community, working with an instructional coach, and partnering with an administrator. Some of the strategies urge you to take action, try something new, or step out of your comfort zone. Others insist that you critically evaluate your belief system. Many will prompt you with questions, challenges, or ideas you'll need to learn about, explain, discuss, or at least *think* about. You needn't attempt these strategies in order, nor should you strive to complete the entire array of tasks included herein. The tasks and reflective questions are labeled alphanumerically for easy reference. Remember: your objective here is to build awareness. Watch, listen, note, observe, record, recognize, study . . . and reflect. So, with that end in mind, let's get started!

Options for Self-Directed Learning. Reflection begins and ends with you. In order to deepen your reflective tendencies, become more aware, increase your intentionality, and build your capacity, you must put forth a concerted effort to reflect often. The big picture is this: we'd like you to think about your job, your teaching, your planning, your goals, your purpose, and your thinking! Try these tasks and consider the following reflective questions—and record your thoughts in your reflective journal (which you'll have prepared after Task A).

Tasks:

A. Begin a reflective journal. Many teachers choose something artsy or classy, though any notebook or note-taking app will do. Research supports the notion that recording your thoughts about a topic can deepen your understanding and perspective on that topic (Hiemstra, 2001; Kerka, 1996; Killion, 1999). In addition, the practice poses numerous health benefits (Pennebaker, 1997). As a first step, start writing whatever thoughts come to mind. Write freely. Write emotionally. Write without worrying about punctuation, hurting people's feelings, being "correct," or any other constraint. Use some of the reflective questions later in this section for guidance if you'd like.

B. For one week, take two minutes at the end of the school day to jot down one success from the day (a WOW!) and something that challenged or surprised you (a YIKES!). These should be quick anecdotes from the day. Just write the date and two short sentences. At the end of the week, glance back at your notes. Can you identify any trends? Continue to journal each day and reflect at the end of each week.

Additional Reflective Questions:

1. Why did you enter the teaching profession?

2. Why do you stay in the field?

3. Describe yourself as an educator. How would you suppose your students would describe you? What would their parents say about you?

4. What are your strengths as a teacher? What are the top three things that you bring to the classroom?

5. When do you feel successful? Can you pinpoint one example in which you were very successful in your teaching? What are the details? To what do you attribute that success?

6. When do you feel least confident? Can you pinpoint one example in which you struggled in your teaching? What are the details? To what do you attribute that struggle?

7. What part of the school day do you look forward to most? Which part do you dread? Why is that?

8. Do you have goals for the year? What are they? How did you come up with those goals? What progress are you making toward your goals?

Options for Student-Focused Learning. Teaching is a people-centered profession. It's also service-oriented. Who are the people for whom we provide this service? Children. Kids. Our students. One way to channel our self-reflective energy is to direct our thoughts onto our students. Why are they the way they are? Are they learning? What do you know about them? How can you better support them? These questions and more drive the following tasks and reflective questions.

Tasks:

A. Grab a class list and that reflective journal of yours. On a fresh page, write *Interests* up top as a title. Now begin to group the students in your class by their personal interests, such as soccer, reading, or animals. If you have difficulty placing a student, simply add him or her to a category titled *Not Sure*. Note that students can be placed in more than one category and all students must be placed somewhere. Once this is complete, start a new page with the title *Reading Levels*, and group your students into new categories. Repeat this process as many times as you'd like. Some other categories you can use include Math Levels, Spelling Levels, Academic Strengths, Academic Struggles, Type of Learner (e.g., Auditory, Visual, Kinesthetic), Social Skills, and Additional Support Groups.

B. (Task B follows Task A, in this circumstance.) Remember that list of students in the *Not Sure* category? Now it's time to return to them and any other students you want to learn more about. Be a detective this week and look for evidence that points to a specific category. It may mean that you have a specific conversation with that student. It may mean that you pull the student aside for some one-on-one time. It may mean that you make some anecdotal notes during a lesson. Whatever you choose, seek to find out as much as you can about the students you know the very least about.

C. Select one student in a class or subject and become an expert on him or her. When is this student successful? When does he or she struggle? How interested is he or she in achieving success in this class or subject? What motivates him or her? What shuts him or her down? Attempt a series of informal experiments. Provide public praise when the student is successful one time, and record how he or she responds. The next time, whisper your praise. How do the responses differ? How are they the same? What does that reveal about the student? Try the same thing by gauging the student's effort, engagement, and success in lessons that are independent, shared with a partner, and done together as a whole class. What can you learn about this student as a learner?

Additional Reflective Questions:

1. Which students are most successful in your class? Why do you suppose they are successful?

2. Which students struggle in your class? Why do you suppose they struggle?

3. When you ask questions in your classroom, who responds?

4. What procedures do you have in place to allow all students to answer your questions?

5. How many students mastered the learning objectives of your last assessment/unit? How many students did not master the learning objectives?

6. What is the difference between a student who is successful and a student who struggles?

7. What role do you play in ensuring the success of every child in your class?

Options for Collaborative Learning. Isolated practice is one of the contributing factors to the gap between what is generally known about good teaching and its actual implementation in classrooms (Bird & Little, 1986). Teaching is no longer a task that we undertake independently. Instead, we are all members of a Professional Learning Community, working collaboratively with our grade-level teams, content departments, or whatever configuration our schools have chosen. In that spirit, we must embrace the notion that our growth is partly the responsibility of our colleagues, just as their growth lies partly on our shoulders. Consider the following tasks and reflective questions while working with your colleagues to enhance your reflective tendencies.

Tasks:

A. Think of the content you are responsible for teaching this year. What—specifically—do you feel the strongest teaching? What subject or topics do you feel the least confident teaching? This week, seek out a trusted colleague who has a similar teaching assignment as you. Intentionally talk with him or her about your areas of strength and areas of concern. What insights did you gain from this conversation? What questions do you still have? How might you add a regularly scheduled conversation with this colleague to your weekly calendar?

B. Select an element of instruction or reflection on which you would like to focus. Ask a colleague if you can visit his or her classroom during part of a prep period. Recruit your instructional coach into the conversation as you plan your visit, identify look-fors, clarify how you will record your observations, and plan your debriefing session with the other teacher. Seeing another teacher put a strategy into play can be enlightening, even if it's not done perfectly.

C. Invite your colleagues to play "Give One, Get One." In this quick activity, each teacher writes a favorite strategy (relevant to a certain topic) on a note card. For instance, a topic may be "on-the-spot intervention ideas." When you and your colleagues meet, you should partner up and explain your strategies to each other. You should then exchange cards and switch partners, so you will be responsible for explaining your original partner's strategy. Repeat as often as you can, and collect a pile of strategies you can take back to try in your own classroom.

Additional Reflective Questions:

1. Which of your colleagues do you respect immensely? Why do you respect him or her? What characteristics do you find admirable in this teacher?

2. Consider an area of strength in your own teaching. What other teacher shares this strength? How can you partner with this teacher to build that strength?

3. Consider an area in which you struggle. What other teacher is strong in this area? How might you partner with this teacher to bolster your skills and knowledge?

4. In your next team meeting, observe the frequency and depth of your colleagues' comments. What are your contributions to team meetings? What do you take away from them?

5. How do you influence the success of your colleagues' students, and how do they affect the learning of yours?

Options for Working with Your Instructional Coach. If you're lucky, you have an instructional coach at your disposal. This coach, if trained in the Continuum of Self-Reflection and the associated coaching strategies from our previous book—*Building Teachers' Capacity for Success* (Hall & Simeral, 2008)—will have specific goals and methods for supporting your reflective growth. First and foremost, your coach will want to partner with you, build an interpersonal relationship, and assure you that the two of you are on the same team. You can also take an active role in the teacher-coach partnership by pursuing some of the tasks and reflective questions that follow.

Tasks:

A. Invite your coach into your classroom to teach a lesson. The content and structure of the lesson aren't important for this task. Instead, you'll be watching the students. When are students most engaged? What are they being asked to do? When are they least engaged? What are they being asked to do? After the lesson, sit down with the coach to discuss your observations. Then create a plan that addresses the lulls in student engagement by infusing movement, a high-interest topic, partner interactions, or another engagement strategy. Again, ask the coach to teach the lesson so you can observe your students. What do you discover? What does this mean for your planning?

B. Ask your instructional coach if he or she will cover your class for 20–30 minutes (or a class period) so you can observe a colleague's classroom. Discuss with your coach what you will be looking for, how you might record your observations, and how this information will help you. Plan the debrief meeting with your coach so all three of you (including your colleague) benefit from this process. Alternatively, if you're willing to visit your colleague's class during your prep period, invite your coach to join you.

C. Ask your coach to process any feedback you receive from your administrator. Most likely, as you'll read in the next section, your administrator will provide very directive, descriptive feedback. Your coach can be an invaluable resource in responding to this feedback with a well-thought-out game plan. Be willing to receive constructive criticism in the spirit it is intended—to help you develop your reflective growth and professional capacity—so you can focus your energy on learning, unlearning, and relearning effective teaching strategies.

Additional Reflective Questions:

1. List the top three struggles you have as a teacher. Share them with your instructional coach. Ask how your coach might support you to better understand and address each of the struggles you identify.

2. With what aspect of daily instruction do you feel the most confident? With what aspect of daily instruction does your instructional coach feel you are the strongest?

3. How can your instructional coach support you? List five ways.

4. How does building awareness of your students strengthen you as a teacher?

5. How does building awareness of your students deepen their learning?

6. What new strategy does your instructional coach believe you should try? Write down everything you already know about this strategy.

Options for Partnering with Your Administrator. Every school has an administrator who has a unique opportunity to provide feedback, guidance, and support to the instructional staff. Your administrator, if trained in the Continuum of Self-Reflection and its associated approach to walk-throughs and tailored feedback from our previous book, will have specific goals and methods for supporting your reflective growth. While working with teachers in the Unaware stage, the administrator's feedback will be directive and specific. You should never be confused about what your administrator expects or would like to see in your classroom. Knowing this, you can build a strong growth-oriented relationship with your administrator by tackling some of the tasks and reflective questions that follow.

Tasks:

A. Be proactive. Ask your administrator to visit your classroom and provide you with specific feedback regarding your practice. It helps if you have a particular request—say, if you would like the administrator to note which students are answering questions aloud during your class and which students never get a chance to do so. This provides a focus for the administrator's observations and limits the amount of variables that come into play. It also helps if your request connects with a schoolwide instructional focus, your content or grade-level team's action plan, or your individual goal.

B. Invite your administrator to read and respond to entries in your reflective journal. In this sense, the journal becomes an interactive journal. (You could also offer this option to your instructional coach or a colleague you trust and respect.) This will require a significant amount of trust, as you'll be opening your thoughts, feelings, and reflections for review and response. If you are comfortable with a little bit of vulnerability, this can be an amazing way to build your relationship and maintain an ongoing dialogue about what's most important—your teaching.

C. If you are unsure of your administrator's expectations, then ask for clarification. It is highly unlikely that you will hit a target you cannot see or one that is moving. It might help to sit down with your administrator and instructional coach together so you can ask the right questions, obtain the proper information, and begin to formulate a plan for putting it into practice.

Additional Reflective Questions:

1. When you write your lesson plans, what elements do you include? What elements do you not include? Why?

2. Consider one lesson you taught today. Why did you choose the instructional strategy you used?

3. Before examining student work, what information do you use to determine whether a lesson was effective? Why?

4. When examining student work, what percentage of students must master the standard or make progress for you to consider the lesson a success? Why?

5. What lesson would you like your administrator to observe and provide feedback on? Why would you choose that lesson?

6. What benefits might result from sharing your reflective journal with your administrator? What problems might arise? When might you meet and talk with your administrator to share your hopes and worries?

7. What does your administrator expect from you regarding lesson plans, instructional techniques, data collection, classroom management, and participation in grade-level or content department meetings? How do you know?

8. What experiences does your administrator have that might enrich your perspective about teaching? When will you set up a time to "talk shop" together?

Pete's Perspective

What first struck me about Mr. Thomas was his enthusiasm for learning and his abundant love of kids. During the interview process, he compelled us to hire him—you can never have too many high-energy, high-enthusiasm personalities on a teaching staff! So he joined our team.

Right off the bat, Mr. Thomas hit it off with his students and colleagues. Affable, personable, and with a great sense of humor, he was living our mission of doing right by kids. Quickly, he settled into some routines that provided order and control in his classroom. I did not receive behavioral referrals from him during the first two months of school, and his students seemed genuinely happy.

During my walkthroughs and early classroom visits, I began to sense that there was something missing. Mr. Thomas was a creature of habit, and he had habitualized some teaching behaviors that did not match his students' needs. He read from the teacher's guide, he asked his students superficial questions, and he was intently focused on covering the curriculum and staying on pace.

In my conversations with him, I provided direct feedback to encourage his willingness to expand his teaching repertoire and modify strategies that were not effective with his students. In my questioning, I pressed him to begin looking at student learning outcomes. Were his students learning? How did he know? Why were students X and Y failing? What strategies could he use to address their struggles?

Mr. Thomas, for the most part, was at a loss. Though he had all the intangible qualities we look for in a teacher, he was lacking some skills and was not well-versed in professional self-reflection. Somewhat embarrassed, he confessed that such scrutiny of results was not part of his training; thus, it was not part of his teaching plan.

His enthusiasm and openness to learning, however, won the day. He proved to be one of the most eager members of the staff, seeking out articles to read, requesting more time with our instructional coaches than anyone else, and begging for additional feedback and suggestions. Though he began the year (and his career) in the Unaware stage, he consciously decided to learn as much as he could as quickly as he could.

At the end of his first year, Mr. Thomas shared, "I learned more this year than I did in all three years of my teacher prep and student-teaching programs combined." The positive results followed.

Conclusion: The Six-Week Challenge

Having read this chapter and tackled some of the strategies listed herein will not, by itself, create an overwhelmingly aware, intentional, reflective educator out of you. However, now that you've embarked on this journey, you're well on your way toward that end.

Remember that your goal as an Unaware-stage teacher is to generate awareness of the need to change and to foster a desire to learn. By doing so, you'll be exiting the Unaware stage and progressing along the Continuum of Self-Reflection to the Conscious stage.

In the meantime, if the wealth of strategies listed in this chapter left you scratching your head and wondering which bite to chew off first, if you prefer a more structured guideline, or if you're feeling strong about your reflective growth and would like to "wrap it up," here is the six-week challenge:

Week 1: Start your reflective journal (Self-Directed Learning, Task A). In it, begin to track your WOW! and YIKES! moments. (Self-Directed Learning, Task B)

Week 2: Select a student in your class and become an expert on him or her. Reflect on how that student succeeds and struggles for a week. (Student-Focused Learning, Task C)

Week 3: Ask a colleague if you can visit his or her classroom to observe a particular instructional strategy. Keep detailed notes on your observations. (Collaborative Learning, Task B)

Week 4: Invite an administrator to visit your classroom and share some feedback about a particular instructional strategy or element of teaching. Record some impressions in your reflective journal. (Partnering with Your Administrator, Task A)

Week 5: Ask your instructional coach to process and game-plan the feedback you've received from your administrator. Write your reflections in your journal. (Working with Your Instructional Coach, Task C)

Week 6: Take a thoughtful walk through your reflective journal. How do your WOW! and YIKES! examples look different this week when compared to the beginning of this journey? Write your reflection down in your journal. If you feel compelled to do so, share your thoughts and feelings on our blog (found online at http://bycfs.edublogs.org). There, you can read other teachers' posts, comment on one another's reflections, and engage in some robust dialogue.

Summary Reflections

As a bonus, here is an additional challenge. Go back and reread this chapter, and then answer the following reflective questions.

1. How has your awareness of your students grown?

2. How has your awareness of content grown?

3. How has your awareness of pedagogy grown?

4. To what degree are your lesson plans more intentional?

5. What impact do you believe you have on student learning?

6. How often do you assess student learning?

7. What strategies do you use to determine whether students learn the intended targets?

8. What actions do you take when you first notice students struggling?

9. How do you plan for these on-the-spot interventions?

10. How frequently are you engaging in self-reflective actions?

The answers to these questions should provide you with ample evidence that you are growing as a reflective practitioner. We commend you for your efforts and energy in this venture, and we encourage you to maintain the continuous push for improvement. Don't worry if you don't recognize the changes just yet. This is often a lengthy process that requires dedication, perseverance, and more than a little bit of good old-fashioned nose-to-the-grindstone labor!

If you'd like, feel free to attempt the various tasks outlined in this chapter multiple times. Ask yourself the reflective questions over and over. There's no such thing as too much of a good thing—the more you practice and strive for improvement, the more you'll grow and progress as a reflective practitioner, which is a great thing! Your continued growth will lead you along the Continuum of Self-Reflection toward the Conscious stage, which is the topic of Chapter 6.

American businessman Olin Miller leaves us with this inspiring quote: "If you realize you aren't so wise today as you thought you were yesterday, you're wiser today."

The Conscious Stage: Is the Knowing-Doing Gap Real?

"The difference between what we do and what we are capable of doing would suffice to solve most of the world's problems."

—Mahatma Gandhi

You have to admit: these days, people know a lot. There is a wealth of information available at our fingertips, and knowledge has never been easier to obtain. With the click of a button, one can find the answer to almost any question, seek expert advice, or learn to make or do nearly anything. Simply put, with just a few searches, queries, or tweets, you can *know* anything.

But that doesn't mean we *do* everything we know. In *The Knowing-Doing Gap,* Pfeffer and Sutton (2000) claim it's *"not* that we don't know what to do. . . . It's that we don't do what we already know" (p.14). The knowing-doing gap suggests a situation in which we—collectively and individually—know what to do but do not act upon that knowledge.

Recently, the Yale Project on Climate Change Communication posted an online piece titled "Do Americans' Actions Speak Louder than Words on Climate and Energy?" Survey information found "a significant gap between Americans' conservation attitudes and their actual behaviors. For example, 88 percent of Americans say it is important to recycle at home, but only 51 percent "often" or "always" do. Likewise, 81 percent say it is important to use reusable shopping bags, but only 33 percent "often" or "always" do (Yale School of Forestry & Environmental Studies, 2010).

The American Heart Association is the nation's oldest and largest organization devoted to both fighting cardiovascular diseases and promoting healthy lifestyles. Founded in 1924, it can easily be touted as one the world's most notable champions for public health. Each year, the association spends millions of dollars to inform the public on topics ranging from what our daily sugar intake should be to warnings about television and its link to poor health, from outlining exercise standards for specific age groups to recommending preventative screenings we all should get. There seems to be no topic the association doesn't address when it comes to building public awareness around personal health.

Come January each year, it's clear that the public is aware and listening to what the American Heart Association has been saying. Losing weight, maintaining a healthier diet, increasing exercise, and quitting smoking continue to stand at the top of people's New Year's resolutions. However, follow-up statistics tell a different story. The University of Scranton's *Journal of Clinical Psychology* determined that after six months, less than half of folks are still working toward their health-conscious New Year's resolutions (Statistics Brain, 2014).

In addition, only 18 percent of people use their gym memberships on a regular basis (International Health, Racquet & Sportsclub Association, 2014), and heart disease and stroke continue to be the leading causes of death among American men and women (Centers for Disease Control and Prevention, 2014). It's remarkably clear: knowledge can only take us so far.

Let's hold up a moment before you dive head-first into a guilt trip about hiding that bag of chocolate. These statistics are alarming, yes, but they also point to the fact that you're not alone. The knowing-doing gap is an epidemic—across cultures, socioeconomic backgrounds, and every cross-section of our society. It can be found on global and corporate levels, and it may well include the districts in which we are employed, the schools in which we work, and the classrooms in which we teach. It's something that affects all of us as educators, no matter how many years of experience or how much expertise we have . . . all of which leads us into this chapter and the exciting work on which you're about to embark.

FIGURE 6.1
The Conscious Stage

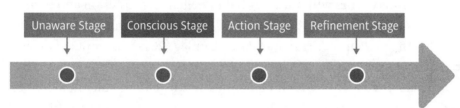

If the results of your Reflective Self-Assessment Tool returned a score in the 15–24 range, that's an indication that you may be operating in the Conscious stage—a term we've coined to describe folks that may find themselves struggling to implement their knowledge into solid, transformative action. In order to see the results we want, we must learn how to put what we know into practice, both intentionally and consistently.

We encourage you to remember that the Continuum of Self-Reflection is a tool we use to help us identify how we think. It gives us a direction for building our self-reflective tendencies and accuracy in a way that will enable us to become more effective decision makers and practitioners in the classroom. There is no value—no "better than" or "worse than"— assigned to any of the stages along the continuum. They're just terms that describe how we think about our work. So let's consider this chapter's focus more closely.

conscious: *being aware of what is around you and having knowledge with the ability to think*

The good news about the "implementation gap," as prominent educational author Doug Reeves calls it (2009), is that we already know what to do. And that's good news indeed! In this stage, you have a knowledge base. You are cognizant of better ways of doing things to bring about positive changes. You have an awareness of needs and the wherewithal to ask for help when necessary.

So Why is Action So Hard?

The dilemma occurs with putting that knowledge into action and turning the action into habits that will bring about longstanding, transformative results. In *The Power of Habit*, Charles Duhigg (2012) attempts to explain the neurological reason behind the choices we make each day and to link our behavior to habits, which he defines as "the choices all of us deliberately make at some point, and then stop thinking about but continue doing, often every day" (p. xvii).

Each decision we make etches out a neurological pathway that, given the right length of time, develops into an unconscious pattern of behavior—not unlike the way that water carves a path as it flows from point A to point B. Take away the water for a period of time and then return it. It will find and follow its original path. "Habits," Duhigg says, "are natural consequences of our neurology" (p.8).

If we take a moment to consider the science, we see that taking action is not what's hard; it's creating a new action in place of an old one where the difficulty arises. Not only do we have to stop the flow of water down a certain path, but we also have to dig a new trench and reroute the water so it flows down the new channel without returning to the old one. It takes an extraordinary amount of energy and time to be successful, which happen to be two precious commodities that teachers have in limited supply.

Meet the Teachers

Consider the implications of this as we visit a couple of classrooms and take a closer look at two teachers who are in the Conscious stage.

Visit 1: Mr. Pickering (secondary): It's 30 minutes before the welcome bell rings, and Mr. Pickering, in his twelfth year of education, is writing his social studies assignments on the board. As he outlines the directions, his mind jumps to the training that he received over the summer on student engagement. It was filled with great ideas, some of which he really wanted to try in his classroom.

This year, however, turned out to be much different than he expected. The very first day was filled with reprimands to put cell phones away and stop talking. He ended up giving an impromptu lecture on what it means to be respectful and assigning extra homework. It seemed to have little impact, as the weeks that followed were filled with more of the same. He knew it was going to be a long year.

Mr. Pickering shrugs to himself as he finishes up. This wasn't the year to offer the reward of "fun learning." He knew it would be a waste of his time. Plus, it took all of his after-hours energy just to keep abreast of the new standards and textbooks they adopted. It was easier to stick with reading directly from the text and assigning the chapter questions when dealing with kids such as these. He'd just wait until next year, when things settled down, to try some new strategies.

Visit 2: Ms. Esteban (elementary): At Friday's collaborative team meeting, the 3rd grade team decides to start Unit 2 on Monday. The weekend flies by, and Ms. Esteban doesn't have a chance to sketch out her lesson plans. She gets to school a few minutes early to figure out what she's going to do for the day. Glancing at the math text, she skims the lesson and decides she'll do what she always does—explain how to do the problem set, model, and have her students complete the practice problems in the book while she walks around to help them.

Math that day is painful—for both the students and Ms. Esteban. Everyone is frustrated, and Ms. Esteban ends up deviating from the plan and teaching a lesson on place value instead. She then assigns the practice problems for homework. She knows that if she had spent more time preparing for the lesson, it probably would have been more successful, but she didn't have the time today.

That afternoon, Ms. Esteban runs into the school's instructional coach who asks how the first lesson of the unit went.

"Horrible," states Ms. Esteban. "My kids are so low in math! They completely lack the basics. I had to explain place value to them today. Some acted like they had never even heard of the hundreds place. We'll continue slogging through the unit, but it's not going to be pretty. I can tell you right now, they're not going to do well on the end-of-unit test."

Characteristics of a Conscious-Stage Teacher

At first glance, it might be difficult to see the common attributes between Mr. Pickering and Ms. Esteban, yet they actually share several. Both are aware that their job is to create meaningful learning experiences for their students, and both see that they are falling short—with class engagement in one and academic struggles in the other. They both have solutions to their problems right in front of them. Mr. Pickering knows of strategies to better engage his students, and Ms. Esteban knows that if her students are low in math, then she needs to be more intentional and strategic in her planning and instruction. They both know they can ask for help from colleagues and site-based instructional coaches.

As Conscious-stage teachers, both Mr. Pickering and Ms. Esteban prefer to accept the current state of affairs instead of taking actions necessary to fix the problem. In Mr. Pickering's case, he chose the comfort of the old way over the risk-taking approach of the new way. It might not work out, so he'd rather play it safe. Ms. Esteban, on the other hand, defaults to a lesson that she is comfortable with after her students respond poorly to her thrown-together lesson. She feared asking for help, since it would mean she'd have to admit that she wasn't fully prepared, which might make her look bad as a teacher.

Referring back to the reflective cycle, let's look a bit deeper at each of the five components of reflection through the lens of a teacher in the Conscious stage.

FIGURE 6.2

The Reflective Cycle

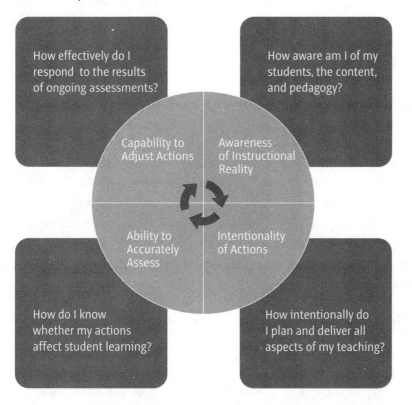

Awareness of Instructional Reality: How aware am I of my students, the content, and pedagogy? Teachers in the Conscious stage recognize that it's important to know their students. They know it's important to keep records and track student progress. When asked, these teachers can move beyond a discussion of student behaviors and address their proficiency as learners. They can quickly describe (in broad terms) students who stand out on a learning spectrum—the best readers, those who learn the fastest, the lowest functioning, and those who seem to struggle with everything. They know that content needs to link to previous learning and can usually explain how an activity connects to something previously taught. They are aware of the need to draw upon new instructional approaches to keep students engaged and are aware of several methods they can try to achieve this. Although they don't often stop to think strategically about it, they can articulate the general needs of their classroom when prompted.

Intentionality of Actions: How intentionally do I plan and deliver all aspects of my teaching? While Conscious-stage teachers may be aware of academic differences among their students, their planning and instruction will not consistently address those differences. This is where the knowing-doing gap shines its brightest, and it is this area—intentionality—that most clearly defines the Conscious-stage teacher. This teacher has awareness of a particular need and may attempt to address it on occasion, but such actions are not implemented consistently. Conscious-stage teachers plan for short-term goals, assignments, and projects; however, long-term and strategic planning do not occur on a regular basis. In this stage, teachers' strategies tend to focus on routines and habits that are well within their comfort zones.

Pete's Perspective

In one of the schools where I was principal, we spent considerable time, energy, and funds to learn about, define, and implement the Workshop Model in our mathematics classes. As a staff, we agreed to pursue this method of instruction in order to raise student engagement rates, critical thinking skills, and overall academic proficiency.

One teacher, Kelly, struggled to embrace this new method. Though she recognized its merits, she had difficulty reconciling the idea that her students could behave appropriately and stay focused on their learning tasks with so much freedom in the classroom. Surely they'd get off topic and wreak even more havoc than they already did.

I worked with Kelly regularly, and—with some trepidation—she launched the Workshop Model with baby steps, first partnering students based on behaviors and then adding very short periods of teamwork via whole-class check-ins. Gradually, she extended the length of the team investigations, realizing that she really only needed to call the whole class together when she spotted several groups making the same errors. She began partnering students based on their academic needs, and she increased the difficulty of the tasks. Eventually, she was able to modify the investigations to extend learning for her more proficient students, thus affording her time to meet intentionally with small groups. This was especially helpful as she allocated time for daily interventions with her most struggling mathematicians.

Later that year, Kelly proudly shared a video of her class engaged in the Workshop Model. The intentionality with which she planned, launched, and modified her work had paid off.

Ability to Accurately Assess: How do I know whether my actions affect student learning? Conscious-stage teachers know they need to regularly assess students and will often follow the easiest path to gather data: relying on weekly assignments and test results to measure whether students understand the content or not. Occasionally, the teacher may ask students to demonstrate their understanding in front of the class or on a whiteboard. Though this is the beginning of on-time assessment strategies, this anecdotal information is not systematically collected, and the teacher has not yet begun to use these data to construct upcoming lessons.

Capability to Adjust Actions: How effectively do I respond to the results of ongoing assessments? Teachers in the Conscious stage tend to remain rather consistent with their teaching strategies, even when students are not learning at high rates. Interventions occur in a reactive manner; if a student is struggling right now, then the teacher may react with an immediate action. Conscious-stage teachers have not yet mastered the art of responding strategically to student misconceptions through deliberate planning, which also includes anticipating mistakes and addressing them before they occur.

Frequency of Reflection: How often do I reflect? Reflection is an intentional, metacognitive act. In the Conscious stage, reflection is often limited to when teachers are grading assignments and scoring exams or when they are prompted by a colleague, an administrator, or an instructional coach. It's also generally limited to after a lesson has been taught or at the end of a unit. A teacher in the Conscious stage may find it easy to identify what is working and what isn't working, though his or her reflective tendencies don't yet delve into the true causes of *why* particular lessons resulted in success or failure. This teacher may hit parts of the reflective cycle (i.e., building awareness, taking intentional action, accurately assessing, and adjusting their work), but it hasn't yet become consistent.

Goal for the Conscious Stage

Knowledge is power when you act on it long enough to create habits that bring long-standing, transformative results. To this end, the Conscious-stage goal is to develop intrinsic motivation and bring consistency into your application of knowledge. You already have a knowledge base and some experiences to lean on, so it's time to make "best practices" intentional and consistent. We want to help build strong new habits—habits that are centered on metacognition, intentionality, and student performance. We want to bring awareness to the strong cause-and-effect relationship between teacher actions and student results in order to motivate you down the path of reshaping habits—a path that will ultimately unlock your professional growth and student achievement.

Growing Along the Continuum

To progress along the Continuum of Self-Reflection is to deepen your thoughtfulness about your professional practice. Having clear targets is a proven effective strategy for enhancing learning, so we've provided clear targets for each of the five key components of the reflective cycle. As you build your capacity as a reflective practitioner, and as you head toward the Action stage, we ask that you consider the following points.

Note Cause-and-Effect Relationships. In the early 1950s, a scientist named Edward Lorenz coined the term *The Butterfly Effect*, which refers to the theory that the flap of a butterfly's wings can cause a small change in the atmosphere, triggering a chain of events that can eventually cause a hurricane in another part of the world (Lorenz, 1963). In order to grow as a reflective practitioner, a Conscious-stage teacher must understand the critical cause-and-effect relationship between teacher decisions and learning in the classroom. Every decision, no matter how large or small, has an impact on students. The more aware we are of how our actions affect our students, the more deliberate we can be in our work.

Plan with Intentionality. Creating better learning opportunities for students is a reflective practitioner's continuous goal. With that end in mind, from the moment you park your car in the school parking lot to the moment you climb back into the driver's seat to leave, you must be intentional in everything you do. You must develop a habit of thinking through the nuances of each daily lesson: How will I engage Samuel? Julissa will finish early, so what open-ended activity can I challenge her with? Yesterday, John struggled with this piece; what scaffolds will I put into place today for him? Questions such as these and more should rattle in your head all day long as you seek to find the best path of learning for your students. The focus should shift from doing what you feel like doing today to doing what you know is best for your students today.

Recognize the Results of Your Actions. As you engage in the act of becoming more intentional in your work, a natural phenomenon will begin to occur—you'll start to notice results! For example, Samuel begins to engage in the lesson and John doesn't seem to struggle as much. Now, rather than waiting until you grade an assignment to determine if students are successfully meeting the learning outcomes, you're listening to a table discussion and looking carefully at students' answers on chart paper. You're asking higher-level questions and reading over shoulders as students process their learning in written form. You're becoming aware of learning in real time, and you're recognizing the cause-and-effect relationship between your actions and your students' success.

Respond to the Needs You See. Just as quickly as you begin to experience learning in real time, you'll find yourself making the necessary adjustments to respond to the needs you see in the same moment. You might realize that the class didn't use the most efficient method to solve an open-ended math problem, so you quickly revise your next steps and ask students to work in table groups to solve the problem using a particular strategy and then compare which method is more efficient. This is thinking on your feet at its finest and leads to the most rewarding results.

Commit to Reflecting Each Day. We don't learn from experience; we learn from reflecting on that experience. Top athletes will record and watch their performances over and over in order to reflect and improve. Building your reflective capacity will not happen by chance. It requires intentional work before, during, and after lessons. Intentional planning sets the stage for learning, and informal assessments are woven into the lesson so you can keep a current pulse on learning and respond in real time. This process frames the work of the reflective practitioner day after day, and the more often it's engaged, the more successes students and teacher will experience. Commit to working through the reflective cycle each day.

Alisa's Approach

My 3-year-old niece learned to swim this past summer. It was a milestone of huge proportions in her home since the process was painstakingly tedious, involving mild hysteria, frustration, and serious high-level negotiations. It literally started with her big toe, and then moved to one foot, a kick, and a "Look Mommy, I'm splashing!" She stalled at this point for three weeks, fearful of going any further.

Where a 3-year-old learns to be afraid of water (when she's been around two older siblings who love to swim) was a mystery to us all. It must be something about venturing into the unknown and (as Maslow would undoubtedly enlighten) the need to feel safe. Only a swimmer knows how swimming feels; a nonswimmer has merely a faint idea.

I'm reminded of the time when I considered changing schools for the first time. A million worries immediately kicked into gear. What if the new principal was tough to work for? What if the culture of the school was negative and isolating? What if I couldn't work with my grade-level colleagues? Bluntly put, I was afraid of how my life might drastically change if I made the decision to "jump all in."

Back at the pool, the second month was filled with more splashes, a graduation to arm floaties, and perpetual cries of "Don't get my face wet!" Hours and hours were logged. Cookie bribes abounded. The last day of summer started with the usual false bravado: "I'll jump off the side if you catch me, Mom," when all of the sudden she leaped. It was several long, breathless seconds before she popped up from the water with a big smile. "I want to do it again!"

Where Do I Start?

"Change is difficult, even when we want to change and are convinced it's worth the effort" (Kise, 2006, p. 4). The fact is, jumping 'all in' is scary. If we don't take the necessary steps to be intentional about the changes we want to make, we may end up standing at the edge of the pool our whole lives. It's time to evaluate and take charge of your situation. So grab a pen and a pad, your favorite laptop or tablet, or whatever your tool of choice is to record your ideas and track your thoughts—the time for action is upon us.

We've compiled a thorough collection of viable strategies designed to increase your reflective habits, including tackling your own self-directed learning, engaging in student-focused analysis, accessing your colleagues within a Professional Learning Community, working with an instructional coach, and partnering with an administrator. Some of the strategies urge you to take action, try something new, or step out of your comfort zone. Others insist that you critically evaluate your belief system. Many will prompt you with questions, challenges, or ideas you'll need to learn about, explain, discuss, or at least *think* about. You needn't attempt these strategies in order, nor should you strive to complete the entire array of tasks included herein. The tasks and reflective questions are labeled alphanumerically for easy reference. Remember: your objective here is to turn your knowledge into solid, transformative action. So, with that end in mind, let's get started!

Options for Self-Directed Learning. "The positive thinker . . . constantly sends out positive thoughts, together with vital mental images of hope, optimism, and creativity," states acclaimed author Norman Vincent Peale (1976). "He therefore activates the world around him positively and strongly tends to draw back to himself positive results" (p. 1). It starts with you, so here, we challenge you to think about your job, your teaching, your planning, your goals, your beliefs, your habits, and your thinking. Try these tasks and consider the following reflective questions—and record your thoughts in your reflective journal (which you'll have prepared after Task A).

Tasks:

A. Begin a reflective journal. Many teachers choose something artsy or classy, though any notebook or note-taking app will do. Research supports the notion that recording your thoughts about a topic can deepen your understanding and perspective on that topic (Hiemstra, 2001; Kerka, 1996; Killion, 1999). In addition, the practice poses numerous health benefits (Pennebaker, 1997). For one week, take two minutes at the end of the school day to jot down one success from the day (a WOW!) and something that challenged or surprised you (a YIKES!). These should be quick anecdotes from the day. Just write the date and two short sentences. At the end of the week, glance back at your notes. Can you identify any trends? Continue to journal each day and reflect at the end of each week.

B. "Habits," author Charles Duhigg states, "are natural conse-quences of our neurology . . . and by understanding how [they] happen, you can rebuild those patterns in any way that you choose" (2012, p. 8). With that in mind, take a closer look at the daily habits you've developed outside of the time you spend with your students. In your reflective journal, generically list what you do each day from the time you arrive at school to when the first bell rings (i.e., before students arrive in class). Now jump to your lunch and/or prep hour and do the same—generically list what you do during that time without students. Finally, sketch out what occurs in the time between the final bell and when you go home. Look back over your lists and consider the following in no particular order. (Feel free to put your thinking on paper as you reflect.)

 ▸ What time do you have to arrive at school in order to feel prepared and ready for the day?

 ▸ What is the first thing you do when you have a free moment during the day?

 ▸ How do you prioritize and keep track of things that need to be done?

 ▸ When do you feel the most productive (e.g., morning, lunch, prep, or after school)?

 ▸ How would you classify your time-management skills?

 ▸ When is the most productive time to create lesson plans?

 ▸ Revisit your list. Are there any habits that pull you away from accomplishing what you need to get done in a day? Highlight the times of your day that you feel could be bet-ter managed.

 ▸ When do you typically reflect on the learning that takes place in your classroom?

C. As teachers in the Conscious stage, there are numerous reasons why we might find ourselves having knowledge but not acting on it. Think of the things you'd like to accomplish in the classroom. What prevents you from putting your knowledge into consistent action? We've outlined a few possible explanations. Journal your thoughts.

▸ *Ambiguity.* The purpose and place for the action is unclear. I need more information before implementing.

▸ *Belief system.* I don't believe that the new action will work and see no need to change. I need to talk more about it with someone and need time to process the change.

▸ *Poor timing.* There are too many things on my plate right now.

▸ *Fear.* I am afraid that my attempt will be unsuccessful and others may judge me. I am afraid that asking for help will show weakness.

▸ *Comfort.* I am comfortable doing what I know.

▸ *Too much work.* I see little reward for the amount of energy required to do this.

▸ *Lack of ownership.* I was not involved in the planning and have little personal investment.

▸ *Lack of trust.* I lack trust in those who are asking me to take action.

D. You may already be able to list a number of actions you'd like to start tackling. You may already be able to identify habits that hinder your ability to follow through on those actions. And you may already be able to pinpoint an additional subconscious reason that is holding you back. It's time to set a short-term, achievable goal. Pick one area of focus, and decide on a goal that will increase your confidence in yourself as a professional.

Determine the actions needed to address that goal and write down the specifics of how you plan to follow through, including who you'll share your goal with for accountability's sake. Use the Quick-Win Goal-Setting Form (Appendix C) to record your goal.

Options for Student-Focused Learning. Siegfried Engelmann, a senior educational specialist at the University of Illinois, states, "If the children aren't learning, we're not teaching" (quoted in Clowes, 2009, p. 13). It's with this in mind that we begin to take a deeper look at our students, who are the very reason we do what we do each day. Why are they the way they are? Are they learning? What do you know about them? How can you better support them? These questions and more drive the following tasks and reflective questions.

Tasks:

A. Select one student who did not master a recent learning objective. Observe this student closely for a day. Sit down and have a conversation with him or her. If possible, watch the student work and ask him or her to explain his or her thinking. Consider your interaction closely. List three needs that this student has. How can you respond intentionally to those needs? What is the result? What cause-and-effect relationships can you identify in this exercise?

B. There are numerous ways to engage students with questioning activities. Today, stick with your typical questioning routine and jot down the names of students who respond and are engaged. Tomorrow, try a new approach. Perhaps you type your questions on a strip of paper, give a different question to different groups of students, and ask them to discuss the questions among themselves before explaining their answers to the class. Maybe you write your questions on sticky notes and place them in various places around the room. Try a random name-generator app to select students to answer questions (it's a modern-day craft-stick strategy). Observe and notice which students respond and are engaged. Compare the results of both strategies. What can be learned? When you adjusted your actions, what results did you see?

C. Assumptions are often made without fully thinking through why we made them. Take a moment to consider and write the assumptions you have about your students. Perhaps there is a particular student (or group of students) with whom you hold varying assumptions. How do those assumptions drive the decisions you make each day? Connect the dots. What cause-and-effect relationships do you see?

Additional Reflective Questions:

1. Which students are most successful in your class? Why do you suppose they are successful?

2. Which students struggle in your class? What specific needs do they have?

3. What adjustments can you make to address those specific needs?

4. When you make adjustments, how do you determine if they were successful moves?

5. Outside of noticing right and wrong answers, what can be learned about a student by looking closer at his or her work?

6. How do students respond when you deviate from your typical approach to teaching and learning?

7. What role do you play in ensuring the success of every child in your class?

Options for Collaborative Learning. Isolated practice is one of the contributing factors to the gap between what is generally known about good teaching and its actual implementation in classrooms (Bird & Little, 1986). Teaching is no longer a task that we undertake independently. Instead, we are all members of a Professional Learning Community, working collaboratively with our grade-level teams, content departments, or whatever configuration our schools embrace. In that spirit, we must embrace the notion that our growth is partly the responsibility of our colleagues, just as their growth lies partly on our shoulders. Consider the following tasks and reflective questions while working with your colleagues to enhance your reflective tendencies.

Tasks:

A. Initiate a conversation with several respected colleagues and pose the following question: What does reflection look like, sound like, and feel like for you? Record their impressions, and don't be afraid to dig deeper to really capture their thinking.

B. Ask a colleague (or your department, content, or grade-level team) to plan a lesson with you. This can be as big or as little as you'd like to make it—you may choose to meet once a week or each day. Indeed, 1 + 1 can equal 3 when people work together. Build synergy as you plan with intentionality around the needs of your students.

C. Ask the same group of people (identified in Task B) if you can analyze student work together. Choose an assignment, quiz, or project, and after scoring the students' work against an agreed-upon rubric, identify a high-, medium-, and low-scoring paper. Bring enough copies for everyone. Analyze the papers' strengths and weaknesses, and engage in a dialogue about how you taught the material to determine why some students might have fallen short of mastery in certain areas. For more ideas of data-driven dialogue structures, there are several wonderful protocols for examining student work in *Protocols for Professional Learning* (Easton, 2009) that we highly recommend.

D. What instructional strategies is your department or grade-level team focusing on? Volunteer to participate in a book study, an article review, or a video analysis of this strategy. Together, select elements of the strategy to try in your classrooms, and then report back on your initial findings. When you're learning together, there's room for error and a safety net when things don't go as planned. Embrace that concept and learn together.

Additional Reflective Questions:

1. Which of your colleagues do you respect immensely? Why do you respect him or her? What characteristics do you find admirable in this teacher?

2. Consider an area of strength in your own teaching. What other teacher shares this strength? How can you partner with this teacher to build that strength?

3. Consider an area in which you struggle. What other teacher is strong in this area? How might you partner with this teacher to bolster your skills and knowledge?

4. In your next team meeting, observe the frequency, openness, and depth of your colleagues' comments. What are your contributions to team meetings? What do you take away from them?

5. How can you share more frequently, openly, and deeply with your colleagues?

6. What staff member do you have the most trustworthy relationship with? How can you utilize that relationship to build accountability around the goals you set?

Options for Working with Your Instructional Coach. If you're lucky, you have an instructional coach at your disposal. This coach, if trained in the Continuum of Self-Reflection and the associated coaching strategies from our previous book—*Building Teachers' Capacity for Success* (Hall & Simeral, 2008)—will have specific goals and methods for supporting your reflective growth. Primarily, your coach will guide your thinking to focus on short-term, fine-grain details. Your common work will include intentional planning, goal setting, and identifying the cause-and-effect relationships between your actions and student learning. You can also take an active role in the teacher-coach partnership by pursuing some of the tasks and reflective questions that follow.

Tasks:

A. Invite your coach into your classroom to teach a lesson. The content and structure of the lesson aren't important for this task. Instead, you'll be watching the students. When are students most engaged? What are they being asked to do? When are they least engaged? What are they being asked to do? Do you notice student responses and behaviors that are different from when you lead a lesson? What is the difference? What is the coach doing or saying that is different? Where does the coach move in the classroom? How does the coach respond to students' questions or comments? Ultimately, your goal is to focus on the cause-and-effect relationships at play. What can you learn from this observation? After the lesson, sit down with the coach to discuss your observations. What might you add to future lesson plans that incorporates some of your learning?

B. Ask your instructional coach to plan a lesson, a series of lessons, or an entire unit together. With the learning outcomes firmly in mind, design activities and assessment tools appropriate for the particular targets. Then deliberately discuss how you will teach the lesson(s). How will you introduce the topic? What strategy will you use to hook students? What background information do you need to preteach? How will you format the instructional delivery, including pacing, regular check-ins, and methods for addressing multiple student learning styles? Ask the coach to observe, coteach, or visit during your teaching. Finally, sit down together to reflect. What worked? What didn't work? Was your planning thorough enough, or do you need to add more details?

C. Ask your coach to help you process any feedback you receive from your administrator. Most likely, as you'll read in the next section, your administrator will keep a very clear and consistent focus on the instructional goals you have set (as an individual, as part of a team, or as part of the entire staff). Your coach can be an invaluable resource in responding to this feedback with a well-thought-out game plan. Be willing to engage in open dialogue in the spirit it is intended—to help you develop your reflective growth and professional capacity—so you can focus your energy on implementing effective teaching strategies consistently and intentionally.

Additional Reflective Questions:

1. What do you believe about how kids learn? What role do you play in the learning process? Ask your instructional coach for his or her point of view, and compare beliefs.

2. What is an instructional strategy you have mastered? How do you know if it's effective?

3. What is an instructional strategy you've heard about but haven't implemented in your classroom? What do you already know about this strategy?

4. How can your instructional coach be of support to you? List 8–10 ways.

5. How does learning a new strategy strengthen you as a teacher?

6. How might implementing a new strategy deepen students' learning?

7. What type of accountability will you need in order to work toward your goal or implement a new strategy successfully?

8. What kind of feedback can you get about a new strategy prior to implementing it in the classroom?

Options for Partnering with Your Administrator. Every school has an administrator who has a unique opportunity to provide feedback, guidance, and support to the instructional staff. Your administrator, if trained in the Continuum of Self-Reflection and its associated approach to walkthroughs and tailored feedback from our previous book, will have specific goals and methods for supporting your reflective growth. While working with teachers in the Conscious stage, the administrator's feedback will consist of reflective prompts that keep you focused on your individual, team, or schoolwide goals—encouraging consistency and intentionality of your actions. Knowing this, you can build a strong growth-oriented relationship with your administrator by tackling some of the tasks and reflective questions that follow.

Tasks:

A. Be proactive. Ask your administrator to visit your classroom often and provide you with specific feedback regarding your practice. The more specific you are in your request, the better. For example, ask your administrator to note which students are answering questions aloud during class or which students never get a chance to do so. This provides a focus for the administrator's observations and limits the amount of variables that come into play. It also helps if your request connects with a schoolwide instructional focus, your content or grade-level team's action plan, or your individual goal.

B. Invite your administrator to read and respond to entries in your reflective journal. In this sense, the journal becomes an interactive journal. (You could also offer this option to your instructional coach and/or a colleague you trust and respect.) This will require a significant amount of trust, as you'll be opening your thoughts, feelings, and reflections for review and response. If you are comfortable with a little bit of vulnerability, this can be an amazing way to build your relationship and maintain an ongoing dialogue about what's most important—your teaching.

C. If you are unsure of your administrator's expectations, then ask for clarification. It is highly unlikely that you will hit a target you cannot see or one that is moving. It might help to sit down with your administrator and instructional coach together so you can ask the right questions, obtain the proper information, and begin to formulate a plan for putting it into practice.

D. Sit down with your administrator to set a short-term goal that relates directly to an area of instructional focus. This could be a schoolwide focus, a strategy your grade-level or department team has adopted, or a technique you have identified as an individual goal. With a clear focus for your work, you can maintain your heading and work toward implementing the chosen strategy with intentionality and consistency. Ask your administrator to visit your class and provide you with feedback and guidance while you're using this strategy; this will allow you to refine and improve your work. Stay the course—the ups and downs often tend to dissuade us from continuing, but perseverance yields the greatest rewards.

Additional Reflective Questions:

1. When you write your lesson plans, what elements do you include? What elements do you not include? Why?

2. Consider one lesson you taught today. Why did you choose the instructional strategy you used?

3. Before examining student work, what information do you use to determine whether a lesson was effective? Why?

4. When examining student work, what percentage of students must master the standard or make progress for you to consider the lesson a success? Why?

5. What lesson would you like your administrator to observe and provide feedback on? Why would you choose that lesson?

6. What benefits might result from sharing your reflective journal with your administrator? What problems might arise? When might you talk with your administrator to share your hopes and worries?

7. What does your administrator expect from you regarding lesson plans, instructional techniques, data collection, classroom management, and participation in grade-level or content department meetings? How do you know?

8. What experiences does your administrator have that might enrich your perspective about teaching? When will you set up a time to "talk shop" together?

Conclusion: The Six-Week Challenge

Having read this chapter and tackled some of the strategies listed herein will not, by itself, create an overwhelmingly aware, intentional, reflective educator out of you. However, now that you've embarked on this journey, you're well on your way toward that end.

Remember that your goal as a Conscious-stage teacher is to begin to implement effective instructional strategies with intentionality and consistency. By doing so, you'll be exiting the Conscious stage and progressing along the Continuum of Self-Reflection to the Action stage.

However, if the wealth of strategies listed in this chapter left you scratching your head and wondering which bite to chew off first, if you prefer a more structured guideline, or if you're feeling strong about your reflective growth and would like to "wrap it up," here is the six-week challenge:

Week 1: Start your reflective journal. In it, begin to track your WOW! and YIKES! moments. (Self-Directed Learning, Task A)

Week 2: Identify your preferred questioning strategy in class and then try a new one. Reflect on students' engagement levels and the manner in which students respond to each. (Student-Focused Learning, Task B)

Week 3: Ask several respected colleagues what reflection looks like, sounds like, and feels like for them. Keep detailed notes on the answers you hear. (Collaborative Learning, Task A)

Week 4: Sit down with your administrator to set a very specific, short-term goal. Clarify the instructional focus and work diligently toward that goal. (Partnering with Your Administrator, Task D)

Week 5: Ask your instructional coach to process and game-plan the feedback you've received from your administrator. Write your reflections in your journal. (Working with Your Instructional Coach, Task C)

Week 6: Take a thoughtful walk through your reflective journal. How do your WOW! and YIKES! examples look different this week when compared to the beginning of this journey? Write your reflection down in your journal. If you feel compelled to do so, share your thoughts and feelings on our blog, found online at http://bycfs.edublogs.org/. There, you can read other teachers' posts, comment on one another's reflections, and engage in some robust dialogue.

Summary Reflections

As a bonus, here is an additional challenge. Go back and reread this chapter, and then answer the following reflective questions.

1. How has your awareness of your students grown?

2. How has your awareness of content grown?

3. How has your awareness of pedagogy grown?

4. To what degree are your lesson plans more intentional?

5. What impact do you believe you have on student learning?

6. How often do you assess student learning?

7. What strategies do you use to determine whether students learn the intended targets?

8. What actions do you take when you first notice students struggling?

9. How do you plan for these on-the-spot interventions?

10. How frequently are you engaging in self-reflective actions?

The answers to these questions should provide you with ample evidence that you are growing as a reflective practitioner. We commend you for your efforts and energy in this venture, and we encourage you to maintain the continuous push for improvement. Don't worry if you don't recognize the changes just yet. This is often a lengthy process that requires dedication, perseverance, and more than a little bit of good old-fashioned nose-to-the-grindstone labor!

If you'd like, feel free to attempt the various tasks outlined in this chapter multiple times. Ask yourself the reflective questions over and over. There's no such thing as too much of a good thing—the more you practice and strive for improvement, the more you'll grow and progress as a reflective practitioner, which is a great thing! Your continued growth will lead you along the Continuum of Self-Reflection toward the Action stage, which is the topic of Chapter 7.

Remember, the knowing-doing gap is real, and you're in charge of it. In the words of Hunter Walk, "Don't try to be the smartest person in the room anymore. The smart person isn't sitting in any room—she's out there getting stuff done" (Walk, 2013).

The Action Stage: What Happens When Art and Science Collide

"The self is not something ready-made but something in continuous formation through choice of action."

—John Dewey

Good recipes should eliminate the possibility of making mistakes, right? In 1896, Fannie Farmer published the world's first "level measurement" cookbook—introducing the concept of standardized measuring spoons and cups to the culinary scene. The book was an instant success and sold out in the first year. Until Ms. Farmer's manual, recipes were written in prose, calling for a "little pinch" of this and "a handful" of that. With the new strict measurement and ingredient system, science was brought into the kitchen for the first time. Ms. Farmer's cookbook, still in print 119 years later, forever changed the way Americans approach food.

Today's recipes still adhere to this model of listing ingredients and specific measurements, but some cooks are now crying that there is too much science and not enough art in the kitchen.

"I think we have gone too far in making recipes too rigid," says cookbook editor and author Judith Jones. "Persnickety details in recipes, such as asking for a specific size onion, mandating fussy ways of cutting vegetables, and listing expensive or hard-to-find ingredients, are frustrating home cooks" (quoted in Shallwani, 2009, para. 10). In other words, cookbooks should teach us how to cook, not just follow instructions. The point of a recipe should be to help us find our own way.

Alisa's Approach

I grew up in a cookie-dough-eating household, where licking spoons, beaters, and mixing bowls was a coveted prize during baking season, which really occurred all year long in my home. My mother was known for her weekly treats. After school, it was not unusual to have a troop of kids stop by the house to raid the cookie jar atop the fridge or have a piece of homemade chocolate cake. Dinner was not complete without a delectable dessert.

Sitting in my kitchen a month ago, I came across a faded recipe card stuck in the pages of an old cookbook. To my surprise, it was Mom's blueberry pie recipe that she'd passed along when I left for college. Instantly, memories came flooding back, and I decided to recreate the dessert. The recipe was simple and easy to follow; an hour later, a delicious-looking pie sat on my counter. On first bite, however, I quickly realized that the pie was not "Mom's." The pie crust was thicker, chewier, and difficult to break with my fork.

I called my sister to complain. Her few, poignant questions offered all the explanation I needed: "Did you chill your butter before cutting it into the flour? You're at a higher elevation. Did you increase the water? How long did you work the dough?" I had clearly followed the recipe, but the pie had not lived up to its full potential because I hadn't made the necessary adjustments that my specific baking situation required.

If the results of your Reflective Self-Assessment Tool returned a score in the 25–34 range, that's an indication that you may be operating in the Action stage—a term we use to describe teachers who are proficient in the science of teaching but need to connect it with the art of making necessary alterations. In the Action stage, we learn when to respond, how to tweak, what specific adjustments to make, and why it's okay to modify at a specific

FIGURE 7.1

The Action Stage

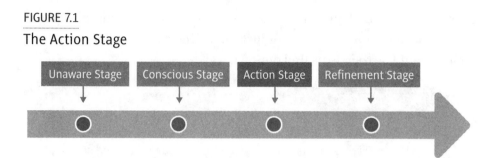

moment in time—all of which brings out the full potential of every child in the classroom.

We encourage you to remember that the Continuum of Self-Reflection is a tool we use to help us identify how we think. It gives us a direction for building our self-reflective tendencies and accuracy in a way that will enable us to become more effective decision makers and practitioners in the classroom. There is no value—no "better than" or "worse than"— assigned to any of the stages along the Continuum. They're just terms that describe how we think about our work. So let's consider this chapter's focus more closely.

> **action:** *the fact or process of doing something, typically to achieve an aim*

In the Action stage, the wheels are rolling and the rubber meets the road. You're inspired, motivated, and working hard to achieve. You are making the effort to do what's best for the kids on a consistent basis. Occasionally, you'll realize a missed opportunity or a lost chance at learning, and it may challenge your confidence in yourself or bring about frustration. You're open and ready to do what needs to be done in order to meet the specific needs in your classroom, and you'll seek out ways to grow your knowledge on your own.

Lights . . . Camera . . .

The first reality of the Action stage is that we've got our goal squarely in front of us at all times: increasing student learning for every child under our care and direction. With such a clear target in focus, we are compelled to do *something* in an attempt to achieve it. John F. Kennedy once clarified our options by stating, "There are risks and costs to action. But they are far less than the long-range risks of comfortable inaction."

Teachers in the Action stage refuse to stand by while their students succeed or fail, while assessments and demographics take control of the narrative, and while education is something that happens to them and their students. They act. They do. They begin to take charge of the outcomes, realizing that they, as teachers, truly are the primary determinant of student success. This commitment is genuine; they begin to build on their "effort optimism"—the sense that if they work hard enough and smart enough, then their students will be able to reach and exceed the lofty goals they set for them.

In short, Action-stage teachers are "in it to win it."

Meet the Teachers

Consider the implications of this as we visit a couple of classrooms and take a closer look at two teachers who are in the Action stage.

Visit 1: Miss Dunn (secondary): Miss Dunn sighed as she glanced at the classwork from the day piled on her desk. Emma was really struggling with the math concepts she was introducing this week. She'd partnered Emma with Joanna today, who she knew could provide solid, in-class tutoring support, and she'd given the class extra time to work through the assignment. She'd also modified the homework for the week. It didn't seem to be working, and she didn't know what else to do. Maybe she'd seek out Mrs. Hannigan, the department head, and ask her advice.

As luck would have it, Mrs. Hannigan was still in her classroom grading papers. Miss Dunn quickly explained the situation with Emma, ending with an emphatic, "I just don't know what else to do for her! Can you give me any advice?" Mrs. Hannigan thought for a moment and then posed the following thoughts for Miss Dunn to consider: "You've told me what Emma can't do. Now explain what she can. In your observations, what basic math concepts does she show evidence of grasping? What strategies do you observe her using as she attempts to solve harder problems? Where in the problem does she get stuck, and what does that tell you about her understanding or lack thereof?"

It was a sleepless night for Miss Dunn as she tossed and turned in realization that she couldn't answer those questions without further observation of Emma. She'd spent so much time helping her work through problems but hadn't known to look for those specific things. She was excited to return to Emma with fresh eyes and further evaluate her specific needs so she could respond appropriately.

Visit 2: Mr. Wilson (elementary): Mr. Wilson was frustrated. Although his mornings usually flowed fairly smoothly, his afternoons were a struggle. It was the third week of school, and his 1st graders seemed to fall apart every day after lunch. He'd tried to structure his math block just like reading—with center rotations so he could differentiate the necessary instruction and keep students engaged in meaningful tasks—but it didn't work. He tried to reinforce students with positive rewards, such as gummy bears for students who stayed on task. He also tried pulling the class back together between rotations for quick check-ins. It did little. James continued to bother the other kids in his group, and Javier refused to do any work at all. It was a constant up and down for Mr. Wilson as he sought to keep everyone engaged while attempting to teach a group at the back table.

Over lunch, he decided what he'd try next. The following day, he'd swap reading for math, running math centers in the morning and reading in the afternoon. It made sense. His class was perfect during reading and had the centers dialed in. Perhaps moving them to the afternoon would work better. He would try anything at this point to find a successful solution.

Characteristics of an Action-Stage Teacher

What do we notice about these Action-stage teachers? Both are committed to do right by their students. Both take immediate action when they see a lack of learning and try multiple methods to solve the problems they encounter. Both are open to new ideas and seek the advice of others. Both are observant, yet perhaps not as tuned in to the details as they could be. Miss Dunn knew Emma was struggling but hadn't really looked closely enough to make an accurate assessment of her specific learning needs. Mr. Wilson, on the other hand, recognized that his class was struggling to engage in the afternoon, but rather than look further into the details of the problem (i.e., Are any students on-task during this time? What is the cause of the off-task behavior?), he makes a blind attempt to solve it, jumping from one solution to the next. Both teachers would benefit from engaging in closer observation and analysis in order to more effectively address the learning situations in their classrooms.

Referring back to the reflective cycle, let's look a bit deeper at each of the five components of reflection through the lens of a teacher who is in the Action stage.

Awareness of Instructional Reality: How aware am I of my students, the content, and pedagogy? Teachers in the Action stage have a solid understanding of their students, inasmuch as they know when learning is taking place and when it is not. They can tell you which students are achieving at what level. They see the big picture and can make daily connections to it. Action-stage teachers can explain what they're teaching and connect it to previous and future learning. They have several instructional approaches in their tool belt and are proficient in their use of them. In fact, Action-stage teachers are often well versed in the technical application of research-based "best practices" in instruction.

FIGURE 7.2

The Reflective Cycle

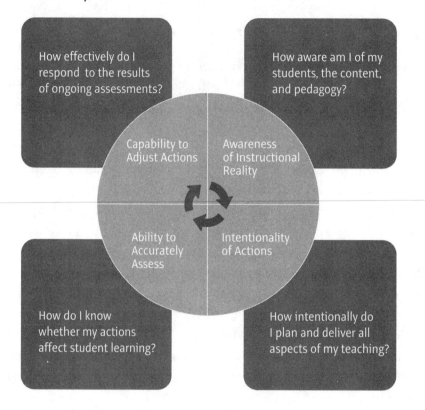

Intentionality of Actions: How intentionally do I plan and deliver all aspects of my teaching? Action-stage teachers are raring and ready to go. They work intentionally toward better engagement, more meaningful instruction, and solid management. It can be easy to become overzealous by overhauling procedures and structures in an attempt to address needs that arise or to jump from solution to solution in search of a better way. Action-stage teachers put an incredible amount of thought into everything that they do.

Ability to Accurately Assess: How do I know whether my actions affect student learning? In this stage, the devil is in the details—the details of observation, that is. Whereas Action-stage teachers are able to articulate whether a student is learning or not, they may struggle to explain exactly what the student knows, what he or she doesn't know, or how he or she knows it. It may be difficult to know what to look for outside of a test or class assignment, and accurately assessing during instruction can prove to be a daunting task. Action-stage teachers may ask students to show work on small whiteboards during a lesson, yet beyond noting who correctly answered a problem and who did not, they're unsure of how to analyze what they see.

Pete's Perspective

One summer, in order to keep my teaching credentials up to date, I enrolled in a math strategies class for teachers at the local university. I figured it would be an easy way to collect three credits and check that box on my application for renewal. Boy was I wrong!

I consider myself a pretty good mathematician, and those who know me understand that I embrace the term *nerd*. However, it became clear very quickly that our professor was not interested in what formulas we knew or what complicated equations we could solve. He was interested in deepening our mathematical reasoning and thinking.

In that class, I found myself addressing his demands of "Prove it," "Why did you take that step?" "Show me," "Are you sure?" "Why do you think so?" "What other options did you have?" and a host of other prompts. However, his tenacity accomplished two tasks: it made my thinking visible so he could better support my learning and it made my thinking visible to me!

That summer, I learned more than just some complex mathematics. I learned methods for engaging my students, my teachers, and my clients in visible thinking—so I could grow as a teacher, leader, mentor, and coach.

Capability to Adjust Actions: How effectively do I respond to the results of ongoing assessments? Action-stage teachers are aware of the learning and non-learning that takes place in their classrooms and naturally want to respond strategically. The response, however, may not address the root of the problem. For example, an Action-stage teacher may notice that several students are struggling to stick with and finish reading an entire book, so he or she may implement a requirement to read at least three books a month and pass the Accelerated Reader quiz for each book. At first glance, this looks like an appropriate response, but further analysis shows that it does not address the real issue at hand. These students might be losing interest in their books because they lack the comprehension skills needed to understand what they're reading. If that's the case, they need specific, guided instruction in the nuances of the book to help build comprehension.

Frequency of Reflection: How often do I reflect? Teachers in the Action stage engage in the act of reflection most successfully before and after lessons. It takes a lot of conscious thought to proceed through the reflective cycle (i.e., building awareness, taking intentional action, accurately assessing, and adjusting their work), and finding the time during a lesson to consciously follow this pattern of thinking can be daunting.

Goal for the Action Stage

Each spring at the Yale School of Medicine, all first-year medical students take a break from their rigorous workloads and file into a nearby art gallery to spend the afternoon looking at 19th century Victorian paintings. As part of a required curriculum, they learn to look for details in centuries-old artwork, practicing a skill that could someday save a patient's life—careful observation and analysis.

Students are asked to diagnose health issues for individuals portrayed in paintings. They should present objective observations and engage in arduous discussion with their peers before drawing any conclusions. To further complicate the scenario, titles and descriptions of each piece of art are covered so students start their observations from scratch and learn that images are not always what they appear to be.

In an age when physicians rely heavily on high-tech imaging and tests, the art of detailed, careful observation and analysis is easily lost. Detecting even the smallest detail can make the difference in coming up with an accurate diagnosis, and the practice of such observations is crucial. "Being a doctor is all about seeing everything that's in front of you—and not just seeing but really looking and watching and observing," former student Kevin Koo says. "To be a better observer is to be a better doctor" (quoted in Dethy, 2009, para. 20).

This same wisdom applies to education. To be a better observer is to be a better teacher, and this weaves directly into our aim for you. The capacity-building goal for teachers in the Action stage is to build experience and strengthen expertise through the development of deeper reflective habits. It starts with detail-oriented observation and an analysis of what you see. We want to help you bring the art and science together in teaching—building confidence around new strategies and insights into your students so you know when to introduce one to the other in order to maximize results in your classroom.

Growing Along the Continuum

To progress along the Continuum of Self-Reflection is to deepen your thoughtfulness about your professional practice. Having clear targets is a proven effective strategy for enhancing learning, so we've provided clear targets for each of the five key components of the reflective cycle. As you build your capacity as a reflective practitioner, and as you head toward the Refinement stage, we ask that you consider the following points.

Zoom in on the Details. Can You Guess the Picture is one of the most popular photo games around. A small part of a larger photo is revealed, and from that information, players have to guess what the entire picture is. In the Action stage, this is often our perspective. We catch a glimpse of student learning through class assignments and assessments and end up trying to guess what the rest of the learner looks like. In order to grow as a reflective practitioner, we must practice taking our observations to an even deeper level and zoom in on the details. What does this student know? What evidence supports my assumptions? What doesn't this student know? From what evidence do I base my information? Was this instructional approach successful? What evidence do I have that supports my conclusion?

Strategize. Once you begin to develop deeper awareness of your students, you can plan with greater intentionality. Consider this scenario: Mr. Hahn's 5th grade class is an unusually energetic group this year. It's clear that many are verbal processors. As a result, Mr. Hahn intentionally plans group activities that require movement and discussion. He strategically sets up discussions so all students are given an opportunity to speak but are also held accountable as listeners. In this manner, Mr. Hahn is able to orchestrate learning in such a way that students are benefitting through their high levels of energy. Planning intentionally now shifts from using this instructional practice because it's a good thing to do to choosing this instructional practice because it's what's best for students at this moment in time.

Consider Student Thinking as You Assess. You've cultivated a deeper awareness of your students and are planning with strategic intentionality to capitalize on their strengths and needs. Now it's time to observe closely and analyze what you see. Rather than look at whether students are getting problems correct or not, you begin to notice the thought processes evident in their explanations and start asking more strategic questions to elicit more sharing of the thinking behind their answers. You're able to more accurately assess the learning while it's taking place—in real time. You can see that although a student might have missed a correct answer, she was on the right track in her thinking and simply needs further examples to cement the learning.

Respond in the Moment. Here's where the art of making necessary alterations comes into play. In real time, just as quickly as you've assessed the thought process of individual students, you're responding—adapting your instruction, questions, and actions. For example, Frank struggles to articulate the main idea, so you respond in the moment and provide a scaffold. "Reread the first paragraph and have a two-minute discussion with those at your table." At the same time, you ask the rest of the class to read on and underline evidence that supports the author's purpose. You then walk over and ensure that Frank's table is able to support him in a way that he'll be able to share with the class when you pull everyone back together. There is no playbook for responsive moves like these.

Develop a Pattern of Reflection. Reflective practitioners have ingrained habits of reflection so they are able, in essence, to make informed snap decisions all day long. These teachers proceed through the reflective cycle in mere seconds. They repeat this cycle a hundred times a day with individual students, small groups, and the class as a whole. They engage in the habit of reflection so often that it happens almost without thinking.

Where Do I Start?

Creating automaticity in your reflections, considering various options, and making in-the-moment decisions can be a challenging task. However, as is the case in any journey, the next step you take is the most important one. But give yourself a little bit of lenience; heed the advice of Ralph Waldo Emerson: "Every artist was first an amateur." The path to artistry in education is before you, and it's your role to travel it earnestly. So grab a pen and a pad, your favorite laptop or tablet, or whatever your tool of choice is to record your ideas and to track your thoughts—the time for refinement is upon us.

We've compiled a thorough collection of viable strategies designed to increase your reflective habits, including tackling your own self-directed learning, engaging in student-focused analysis, accessing your colleagues within a Professional Learning Community, working with your instructional coach, and partnering with an administrator. Some of the strategies urge you to take action, try something new, or step out of your comfort zone. Others insist that you critically evaluate your belief system. Many will prompt you with questions, challenges, or ideas you'll need to learn about, explain, discuss, or at least *think* about. You needn't attempt these strategies in order, nor should you strive to complete the entire array of tasks included herein. The tasks and reflective questions are labeled alphanumerically for easy reference. Remember: your objective here is to build experience and strengthen expertise through the development of deeper reflective habits. So, with that end in mind, let's get started!

Options for Self-Directed Learning. Reflection starts and ends with you. Here, we'd like you to think about your job, your teaching, your planning, your goals, your purpose, and your thinking! Try these tasks and consider the embedded reflective questions—and record your thoughts in your reflective journal (which you'll have prepared after Task A).

Tasks:

   A. Begin a reflective journal. Many teachers choose something artsy or classy, though any notebook or note-taking app will do. Research supports the notion that recording your thoughts about a topic can deepen your understanding and perspective on that topic (Hiemstra, 2001; Kerka, 1996; Killion, 1999). In addition, the practice poses numerous health benefits (Pennebaker, 1997). For one week, take two minutes at the end of the school day to jot down one success from the day (a WOW!) and something that challenged or surprised you (a YIKES!). These should be quick anecdotes from the day. Just write the date and two short sentences. At the end of the week, glance back at your thoughts. What do you notice about your thinking? Continue to journal each day and reflect at the end of each week.

   B. Let's take a closer look at strategic planning. Grab your lesson plans for the past week. Select one lesson to examine in greater depth, and journal your reflection around the following questions. When did you plan for that lesson? How did you decide on it? What factors did you consider as you wrote it in your lesson planner? You likely have particular instructional strategies that you use often and are comfortable implementing in your classroom. What specific strategies shaped that lesson? Did you consider alternative strategies? How did you decide which strategy to include in your planning?

C. Describe your beliefs about how students learn. Do you adhere to a constructivist model, where students engage primarily in group work and take more ownership of learning, or do you subscribe to a directed instruction model, where you predominantly teach what needs to be learned while students practice independently? How does your belief system influence the way you strategize instruction? Are there particular lessons that dictate your instructional techniques, the selection of activities, and the assessment tools you'll use? How do you reconcile the learning goals with your beliefs about how students learn?

Options for Student-Focused Learning. Teaching is a people-centered profession. It's also service-oriented. Who are the people for whom we provide this service? Children. Kids. Our students. One way to channel our self-reflective energy is to direct our thoughts onto our students. Why are they the way they are? Are they learning? What do you know about them? How can you better support them? These questions and more drive the following tasks and reflective questions.

Tasks:

A. Grab a class list and that reflective journal of yours. Let's delve deeper into the specific individuals who make up your community of learners. Select one student in a class or subject on whom you'll become an expert. When is this student successful? When does he or she struggle? How interested is he or she in achieving success in this class or subject? What motivates him or her? What shuts him or her down? Attempt a series of informal experiments. Provide public praise when the student is successful one time, and record how he or she responds. The next time, whisper your praise. How do the responses differ? How are they the same? What does that reveal about the student? Try the same thing by gauging the student's effort, engagement, and success in lessons that are independent, shared with a partner, and done together as a whole class. What can you learn about this student as a learner?

B. Select one student who did not master the most recent learning objectives. Go back and review the topics, instructional strategies you used, assignments, quizzes, projects, and curriculum. What types of mistakes is he or she making? What does the evidence tell you about what he or she might know in relation to the objective? Sit down and have a conversation, and perhaps ask the student to explain his or her thinking to you. What insights does he or she provide? Do you notice any trends or patterns in the student's thinking? How might you use that information in the future? What intervention strategies might you now attempt?

C. Invite your instructional coach, a department head, or a trusted peer into your classroom to teach a lesson. The content and structure of the lesson aren't important; concentrate on watching the students. When are students most engaged? What are they being asked to do? When are they least engaged? What are they being asked to do? As they engage in the lesson, what evidence can you gather that reveals the thinking behind their actions? Now look closely at your visiting guest teacher. What evidence do you see of him or her taking advantage of each learning opportunity that presents itself? What evidence of "responding in the moment" do you see?

Additional Reflective Questions:

1. Which instructional tasks provide the best opportunities to elicit informal assessment of student thinking?

2. What type of teacher-driven questions lead students to explain their thinking?

3. How do errors show what students know?

4. Do I notice any patterns or trends in student thinking that need to be addressed?

5. When a particular student struggles, is the inaccuracy at a conceptual, application, or procedural level?

6. Are students making errors or struggling in ways that I could have predicted?

7. What scaffolds need to be in place in order to make an individual student successful?

8. What opportunities can I seek that allow me to provide on-the-spot interventions?

Options for Collaborative Learning. Isolated practice is one of the contributing factors to the gap between what is generally known about good teaching and its actual implementation in classrooms (Bird & Little, 1986). Teaching is no longer a task that we undertake independently. Instead, we are all members of a Professional Learning Community, working collaboratively with our grade-level teams, content departments, or whatever configuration our schools embrace. In that spirit, we must embrace the notion that our growth is partly the responsibility of our colleagues, just as their growth lies partly on our shoulders. Consider the following tasks and reflective questions while working with your colleagues to enhance your reflective tendencies.

Tasks:

A. Ask a colleague if you can visit his or her classroom during part of a prep period, and watch him or her teach. Recruit your instructional coach into the conversation as you plan your visit. Identify the look-for: how your colleague responds in the moment to address specific needs that arise. Clarify how you will record your observations and plan your debriefing session with the other teacher. Seeing another teacher put a strategy into play can be very enlightening, even if it's not done perfectly.

B. Ask a colleague (or your department, content, or grade-level team) if you can analyze student work together. Choose an assignment, a quiz, or a project, and after scoring the students' work against an agreed-upon rubric, identify a high-, medium-, and low-scoring paper. Bring enough copies for everyone. Analyze the papers' strengths and weaknesses, and engage in a dialogue about how you taught the material to determine why some students might have fallen short of mastery in certain areas. For more ideas of data-driven dialogue structures, there are several wonderful protocols for examining student work in *Protocols for Professional Learning* (Easton, 2009) that we highly recommend.

C. What instructional strategies is your department or grade-level team focusing on? Spearhead a movement to engage in a book study, an article review, or a video analysis of this strategy. Together, select elements of the strategy to try in your class-rooms, and then report back on your initial findings. When you're learning together, there's room for error and a safety net when things don't go as planned. Embrace that concept and learn together.

Additional Reflective Questions:

1. Which of your colleagues do you respect immensely? Why do you respect him or her? What characteristics do you find admirable in this teacher?

2. Consider an area of strength in your own teaching. What other teacher shares this strength? How can you partner with this teacher to build that strength?

3. Consider an area in which you struggle. What other teacher is strong in this area? How might you partner with this teacher to bolster your skills and knowledge?

4. What is an area of instruction you'd like to learn more about? Why is that appealing to you?

5. In your next team meeting, observe the frequency and depth of your colleagues' comments. What are your contributions to team meetings? What do you take away from them?

6. How do you influence the success of your colleagues' students, and how do they affect the learning of yours?

Options for Working with Your Instructional Coach. If you're lucky, you have an instructional coach at your disposal. This coach, if trained in the Continuum of Self-Reflection and the associated coaching strategies from our previous book—*Building Teachers' Capacity for Success* (Hall & Simeral, 2008)—will have specific goals and methods for supporting your reflective growth. For the most part, your coach will be expanding your repertoire of skills, encouraging you to try new strategies and spread your wings, and asking you a lot of reflective questions to prompt your thinking. You can also take an active role in the teacher-coach partnership by pursuing some of the tasks and reflective questions that follow.

Tasks:

A. Your instructional coach will ask you if there's anything you need to be more successful. Be prepared with a couple of options. Perhaps the coach can coteach a lesson with you, helping to capitalize (in the moment) on every instructional opportunity that arises in your lesson. It can be powerful to have a second set of eyes. You might also ask the coach to model a specific instructional technique for you, allowing you to sit back and observe students closely during learning. Keep your eyes wide open during this opportunity. What moments does the coach capitalize on (or miss) that might be chances to enhance student learning? What interventions does the coach slide into the lesson on the fly? How might you incorporate similar structures into your planning and lesson delivery? Debrief with your coach after the lesson.

B. Ask your instructional coach if he or she will cover your class for 20–30 minutes (or a class period) so you can observe a colleague's classroom. Discuss with your coach what you will be looking for, how you might record your observations, and how this information will help you. Plan the debrief meeting with your coach so all three of you (including your colleague) benefit from this process. Alternatively, if you're willing to visit your colleague's class during your prep period, invite your coach to join you.

C. Ask your coach to process any feedback you receive from your administrator. Most likely, as you'll read in the next section, your administrator will offer you a multitude of open-ended, reflective prompts. Your coach can be an invaluable resource in contemplating these questions, considering alternatives, and researching possible responses. Your administrator's prompting is designed to do one thing: deepen your thinking and expand your instructional horizons. Use your coach to banter, to weigh, to debate, and to hypothesize. Your reflection—and your teaching—will grow accordingly.

D. Analyze video of your teaching with your instructional coach. Though this might feel uncomfortable at first (we suggest you watch the video alone the first time, just to get through the awkwardness of it), having someone next to you expands the scope of what you're able to notice. If you have clear look-fors, keep those in mind to focus your observations further. What do you see? How do students respond to certain actions and teaching strategies? Can you pinpoint specific steps you took that led to student learning? Alternatively, can you cite specific actions that impeded student learning? Add this knowledge to your planning regimen.

Additional Reflective Questions:

1. What do you believe about how kids learn? What other theories are out there that you might investigate to broaden your knowledge base?

2. What is an instructional strategy you have mastered? How do you know if it's effective?

3. What is an instructional strategy you've heard about but haven't implemented in your classroom? What do you already know about this strategy?

4. How can your instructional coach be of support to you? List 8–10 ways.

5. How does learning a new strategy strengthen you as a teacher?

6. How might implementing a new strategy deepen students' learning?

7. What kind of feedback can you get about a new strategy prior to implementing it in the classroom?

8. How do more detailed observations help you strategize when lesson planning?

9. How do more detailed observations drive your in-the-moment responses?

Options for Partnering with Your Administrator. Every school has an administrator who has a unique opportunity to provide feedback, guidance, and support to the instructional staff. Your administrator, if trained in the Continuum of Self-Reflection and its associated approach to walkthroughs and tailored feedback from our previous book, will have specific goals and methods for supporting your reflective growth. While working with teachers in the Action stage, the administrator's feedback is almost entirely composed of open, reflective questions. In this sense, your administrator is encouraging your thirst for knowledge, your willingness to try new approaches, and your awareness of the impact of your actions. Knowing this, you can build a strong growth-oriented relationship with your administrator by tackling some of the tasks and reflective questions that follow.

Tasks:

A. Be proactive. Ask your administrator to visit your classroom and provide you with specific feedback regarding your practice. The more specific you are in your request, the better. For example, ask your administrator to note which students are answering questions aloud during class and which students never get a chance to do so. This provides a focus for the administrator's observations and limits the amount of variables that come into play. It also helps if your request connects with a schoolwide instructional focus, your content or grade-level team's action plan, or your individual goal.

B. Invite your administrator to read and respond to entries in your reflective journal. In this sense, the journal becomes an interactive journal. (You could also offer this option to your instructional coach or a colleague you trust and respect.) This will require a significant amount of trust, as you'll be opening your thoughts, feelings, and reflections for review and response. If you are comfortable with a little bit of vulnerability, this can be an amazing way to build your relationship and maintain an ongoing dialogue about what's most important—your teaching.

C. If you are unsure of your administrator's expectations, then ask for clarification. It is highly unlikely that you will hit a target you cannot see or one that is moving. It might help to sit down with your administrator and instructional coach together so you can ask the right questions, obtain the proper information, and begin to formulate a plan for putting it into practice.

D. Ask your administrator for opportunities to learn, grow, and expand your knowledge. This might mean suggesting a membership to a local or national education organization (such as ASCD or Learning Forward), acquiring a subscription to a respected education journal (such as *Educational Leadership*), or attending a national education conference. Identify a few professional books you'd like to read this year, and suggest that the school budget cover multiple copies of each one—for the administrator, coach, and other interested colleagues to read together—in order to build common knowledge. The more you learn, the more you can implement, and the more your students will benefit.

Additional Reflective Questions:

1. When you write your lesson plans, what elements do you include? What elements do you not include? Why?

2. Consider one lesson you taught today. Why did you choose the instructional strategy you used?

3. Before examining student work, what information do you use to determine whether a lesson was effective? Why?

4. When examining student work, what percentage of students must master the standard or make progress for you to consider the lesson a success? Why?

5. What lesson would you like your administrator to observe and provide feedback on? Why would you choose that lesson?

6. What benefits might result from sharing your reflective journal with your administrator? What problems might arise? When might you talk with your administrator to share your hopes and worries?

7. What does your administrator expect from you regarding lesson plans, instructional techniques, data collection, classroom management, and participation in grade-level or content department meetings? How do you know?

8. What experiences does your administrator have that might enrich your perspective about teaching? When will you set up a time to "talk shop" together?

Conclusion: The Six-Week Challenge

Having read this chapter and tackled some of the strategies listed herein will not, by itself, create an overwhelmingly aware, intentional, reflective educator out of you. However, now that you've embarked on this journey, you're well on your way toward that end.

Remember that your goal as an Action-stage teacher is to build experience and strengthen expertise through the development of deeper reflective habits. By doing so, you'll be exiting the Action stage and progressing along the Continuum of Self-Reflection to the Refinement stage.

In the meantime, if the wealth of strategies listed in this chapter left you scratching your head and wondering which bite to chew off first, if you prefer a more structured guideline, or if you're feeling strong about your reflective growth and would like to "wrap it up," here is the six-week challenge:

Week 1: Start your reflective journal. In it, begin to track your WOW! and YIKES! moments. (Self-Directed Learning, Task A)

Week 2: Select a student in your class who did not master the most recent learning objective. Spend time analyzing his or her work and/or talking to the student about his or her thinking. (Student-Focused Learning, Task B)

Week 3: Ask a colleague if you can visit his or her classroom to observe how he or she responds in the moment to address specific needs that arise during the lesson. Keep detailed notes on your observations. (Collaborative Learning, Task A)

Week 4: Invite your administrator to "share the pen" in your reflective journal. Having a spot where you share thoughts, questions, ideas, and wonderings can be a powerful learning mechanism. (Partnering with Your Administrator, Task B)

Week 5: Ask your instructional coach to teach a lesson in your class so you can watch for opportunities to provide in-the-moment interventions. Write your reflections in your journal. (Working with Your Instructional Coach, Task A)

Week 6: Take a thoughtful walk through your reflective journal. How do your WOW! and YIKES! examples look different this week when compared to the beginning of this journey? Write your reflection down in your journal. If you feel compelled to do so, share your thoughts and feelings on our blog, found online at http://bycfs.edublogs.org/. There, you can read other teachers' posts, comment on one another's reflections, and engage in some robust dialogue.

Summary Reflections

As a bonus, here is an additional challenge. Go back and reread this chapter, and then answer the following reflective questions.

1. How has your awareness of your students grown?

2. How has your awareness of content grown?

3. How has your awareness of pedagogy grown?

4. To what degree are your lesson plans more intentional?

5. What impact do you believe you have on student learning?

6. How often do you assess student learning?

7. What strategies do you use to determine whether students learn the intended targets?

8. What do you do when you first notice students struggling?

9. How do you plan for these on-the-spot interventions?

10. How frequently are you engaging in self-reflective actions?

The answers to these questions should provide you with ample evidence that you are growing as a reflective practitioner. We commend you for your efforts and energy in this venture, and we encourage you to maintain the continuous push for improvement. Don't worry if you don't recognize the changes just yet. This is often a lengthy process that requires dedication, perseverance, and more than a little bit of good old-fashioned nose-to-the-grindstone labor!

If you'd like, feel free to attempt the various tasks outlined in this chapter multiple times. Ask yourself the reflective questions over and over. There's no such thing as too much of a good thing—the more you practice and strive for improvement, the more you'll grow and progress as a reflective practitioner, which is a great thing! Your continued growth will lead you along the Continuum of Self-Reflection toward the Refinement stage, which is the topic of Chapter 8.

As you become more reflective and your practice shifts from the science of teaching to the art of ensuring learning, keep the words of Albert Einstein in your head: "After a certain high level of technical skill is achieved, science and art tend to coalesce in esthetics, placidity, and form. The greatest scientists are always artists as well."

The Refinement Stage:
Smoothing Out the Rough Edges

*"Follow effective action with quiet reflection. From the quiet
reflection will come even more effective action."*

—Peter Drucker

Have you ever watched a Denver Broncos game and marveled (or laughed uncomfortably) at quarterback Peyton Manning's arm waving, yelling, pointing, gesticulating routine at the line of scrimmage? Have you ever wondered why he continuously seems to yell "Omaha" or "Alley" or some other code words prior to running a play?

These histrionics are neither an act of showmanship nor a random collection of dance moves. Rather, Manning has stepped up to the line of scrimmage, surveyed the defense, analyzed their formation, determined how they tend to use that formation, decided that the play he had already selected might not work against that defense, and used his arms, voice, and codes to call an "audible"—football jargon for choosing a new play right there on the spot.

What football fans (die-hard or casual) see on TV is #18 yelling and waving and then taking the hike and running a play. If his career record is any indication (he holds multiple records for touchdowns, yards gained, quarterback rating, and others), Manning's audibles are wildly successful.

He holds five NFL MVP awards, but he'll be the first to tell you that he's neither the strongest, fastest, or most athletically gifted player on the field. So what gives?

Quite simply, he's a ravenous thinker. He pays attention not only to his team's plays and players but also to the plays and tendencies of his opposition. His preparation and planning routines are legendary. He watches hours of gameplay footage prior to taking the field. Every play he runs is done very deliberately; he leaves nothing to chance. After scores or between quarters, you'll find him on the sidelines scrutinizing photos of defensive arrangements and offensive schemes as he determines what's working and what needs to be changed. And he calls audibles. Lots of audibles.

Snap Decisions

We make hundreds, if not thousands, of snap decisions (football pun intended) every day—how long to brush our teeth, what to eat for breakfast, how to respond to a friend's e-mail, and which birthday card to purchase. Our intuitive judgment is developed by experience, training, knowledge, and repetition. Our brain collects information and commits it to memory that can be drawn upon at a later time. "Eventually," says science journalist Amanda Rose Martinez, "through constant practice, you get to the point where . . . these processes get pushed down into the subconscious. They don't need to be consciously worked out anymore. They become a subroutine" (Martinez, 2010, para. 14).

Take driving, for example. At the very beginning, the act of getting into a vehicle, turning the key in the ignition, and putting it into gear takes deliberate, conscious thinking. Over time, however, repetition moves those actions to our subconscious, and we no longer have to make a conscious effort. Often, after reaching our destinations, we find that we can't remember the slowing down to avoid a rock in the road, the cars we passed, or the bumps we crossed on the way. And just like in driving, reflective practitioners in the classroom have developed natural habits of reflection so they are able, in essence, to think without thinking. That is, they can make snap decisions about teaching and students in mere seconds.

FIGURE 8.1
The Refinement Stage

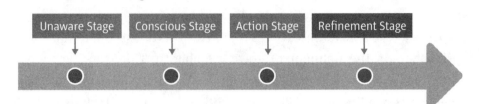

If the results of your Reflective Self-Assessment Tool returned a score in the 35–40 range, that's an indication that you may be operating in the Refinement stage—a term we use to describe teachers who think critically throughout their day, continuously reflect on their practice, and dial in to the learning that is taking place in each moment of every day. These teachers are highly motivated, knowledgeable about best-practice strategies, and adept at turning the science of teaching into a beautiful art.

We encourage you to remember that the Continuum of Self-Reflection is a tool we use to help us identify how we think. It gives us a direction for building our self-reflective tendencies and accuracy in a way that will enable us to become more effective decision makers and practitioners in the classroom. There is no value—no "better than" or "worse than"— assigned to any of the stages along the Continuum. They're just terms that describe how we think about our work. So let's consider this chapter's focus more closely.

refinement: *improvement or clarification of something by making small changes*

When you refine something, you make it better. Whether it's a recipe, manners, an essay, or classroom instruction, refinement requires identifying and fixing its flaws in an attempt to improve, clarify, or perfect results. The Refinement-stage teacher's classroom, like all classrooms, is not perfect. Students still struggle, behavioral problems still arise, the teacher still experiences uncertainty, and the learning process is still not linear or direct. The class is filled with the same challenges as everyone else's. The difference is twofold: it is the way the teacher sees the challenges and the way the teacher intervenes that make this classroom unique.

Teachers in the Refinement stage are able to "think on their feet." They know when to push and when to pull back. They know that one best-practice strategy may not meet the needs of every learner in the classroom, and they understand there may be times when a best-practice strategy will not work. In our previous book, we describe the following scenario:

> Refinement teachers stand in front of a classroom of 25 children and see 25 unique individuals bringing 25 different experiences and perspectives to the table. They see 25 distinct personality and learning styles, each defined by diverse strengths and weaknesses. There is no perfect research or study that can tell Refinement teachers exactly what strategies will meet the unique needs of every child who walks in the door, but these teachers don't look for one that will. They know that in a classroom full of children, the variables are endless. (Hall & Simeral, 2008, p. 93)

Meet the Teachers

Consider the implications of this as we visit a couple of classrooms and take a closer look at two teachers who are in the Refinement stage.

Visit 1: Mr. Torres (secondary): "I want you to watch a very brief video of a man stacking coins in fast motion," Mr. Torres tells his Algebra II class. "As you watch, please write down the first question that comes to your mind. *[Three minutes later.]* Great! I'm curious what questions are out there, so throw some out to me." He proceeds to write the questions on the board. "Now, talk in your groups, share your question with the others, and decide, as a team, which question from your group you find the most interesting." Mr. Torres then listens to the conversations of each of the prearranged teams of four.

"Now," he continues, after making a few handwritten notes of student comments, "your team is charged with two more tasks. As a group, guess a correct answer to your question, and determine what an incorrect answer would look like." He continues to walk around the room, listening in on conversations and taking anecdotal notes. At this point, Mr. Torres highlights a question he previously heard—one that specifically addresses the standards he has built this unit around.

"Now, I'd like you to consider this question. As a team, decide what elements are important and what strategies could be used to solve the problem. Each of you has a different colored marker. Explain your thinking on the chart paper in front of you. Everyone must show participation in some way. Andrew, Marcus, Coral, and Annalise, please meet me at the back of the room."

While the class is working on the posters, Mr. Torres quickly gathers four students who need concrete examples to build conceptual understanding to begin stacking pennies on the back table. He then sees that one table group is arguing over a strategy. He pops over, listens to the heated discussion, and poses a few clarifying questions to guide their thinking down the right path. He then returns to the students in the back of the room to provide some explicit small-group instruction.

After the lesson is over, Mr. Torres explains, "I believe in inquiry-based learning. With math, that's the only way to engage students who have preconceived notions about themselves as mathematicians. Tomorrow, I'll formalize and consolidate the math expressed today, reconcile conflicting ideas, and finally ask students to provide a title that would summarize the entire lesson. Then I offer my own. It's not always perfect, but I learn so much about my students' thinking through this approach and am better able to specifically address misconceptions that arise right on the spot."

Visit 2: Mrs. Phung (elementary): It's writing time in Mrs. Phung's 2nd grade class, and everyone pulls out his or her personal journal. Mrs. Phung projects hers (decorated with pictures of her family) and proceeds to think aloud as she writes about her weekend trip to the lake. Today, she wants to introduce her students to writing with more details (part of the narrative writing lesson she's going to be doing later that afternoon), so she makes sure to model explicit descriptions of the sights and smells she experienced. After a few minutes, she looks up in mock surprise. "Oh my goodness! I forgot that you haven't started writing yet! I was so caught up in thinking about this beautiful place and was so excited to paint the picture using descriptive words. Please, please go ahead and begin writing. Don't let me keep you waiting!"

With that, she takes her journal and moves to Christopher's desk. "Christopher, do you mind if I sit next to you today to write?" Christopher shakes his head and goes back to staring at his blank page. After a few moments of writing more in her journal, Mrs. Phung quietly leans over, "Are you struggling to think of a topic today?" Christopher nods his head. "Do you remember last week when I was struggling to come up with an idea? Do you remember what I did?"

Francine calls out from her desk next to Christopher's, "you wrote a list of your favorite things."

Mrs. Phung smiles and says, "Maybe you can think of a list to write."

"My favorite thing is Pokemon." Christopher says.

"I don't know much about Pokemon," Mrs. Phung shares. "Perhaps you can list the different characters and describe them for me so I have a better idea." Christopher's eyes light up as he picks up his pencil to write.

Mrs. Phung then scoots over to another table to intentionally use proximity to keep students on task. She checks in with Andrea, a struggling writer who has what appears to be a jumbled mix of letters on her page. Andrea is able to read what she wrote, and Mrs. Phung immediately asks her to be the first to share during rug time. Fifteen minutes later, she pulls the class together. As various students share their work from the day, Mrs. Phung asks pointed questions to draw out how students decided what to write and the thinking that went into picking choice detail words.

Mrs. Phung explains, "I use a 15-minute writing time each morning to identify specific minilessons that will drive my formal writing instruction later in the day. Journaling provides a window into student thinking and helps me get to know my students in a deeper way."

Characteristics of a Refinement-Stage Teacher

What do we notice about these Refinement-stage teachers? Both operate under a constructivist belief about teaching. They empower students to take ownership of their learning, while they work as facilitators. Both are skilled at crafting tasks that elicit student thinking and group discussion—tasks that will give them insight into student understanding and misconceptions. Both are working toward clear learning outcomes but make allowances for slight deviations to address specific needs that arise during a lesson. Both Mr. Torres and Mrs. Phung have the ability to think on their feet, and both move through the reflective cycle (i.e., building awareness, intentionally responding, accurately assessing, and adjusting their actions) in mere seconds, over and over throughout the day. If asked to explain why they do what they do, they might find it difficult to articulate. Nevertheless, with further probing, it would be possible to see that there is a rationale behind every decision they make, no matter how small.

Referring back to the reflective cycle, let's look a bit deeper at each of the five components of reflection through the lens of a teacher in the Refinement stage.

Awareness of Instructional Reality: How aware am I of my students, the content, and pedagogy? Teachers in the Refinement stage strive to see students in terms of strengths, not deficits. They understand that teaching is not about learning every research-based best practice or knowing all the "rules" to good instruction; rather, it is about understanding the individual

FIGURE 8.2

The Reflective Cycle

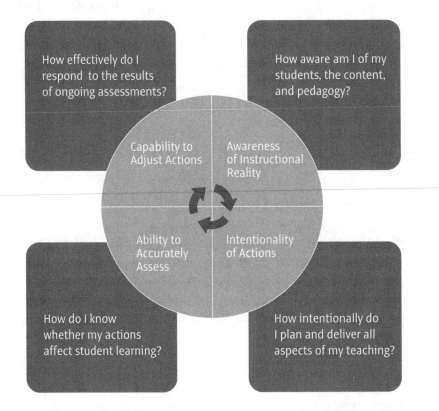

How effectively do I respond to the results of ongoing assessments?

How aware am I of my students, the content, and pedagogy?

Capability to Adjust Actions

Awareness of Instructional Reality

Ability to Accurately Assess

Intentionality of Actions

How do I know whether my actions affect student learning?

How intentionally do I plan and deliver all aspects of my teaching?

child with whom they are working and discovering what that child needs to be successful. In other words, they connect the right strategy to the right student to optimize learning. These practitioners are attuned to every nuance in the classroom, from Joel, who needs extra time to process before speaking, to Sara, who needs to speak in order process her learning. This teacher has a solid understanding of the content that needs to be taught, what his or her students know and don't know, and what pedagogical approach will best help them learn.

Intentionality of Actions: How intentionally do I plan and deliver all aspects of my teaching? A Refinement-stage teacher will carefully orchestrate all of his or her lessons. This teacher will arrange tasks, engagement activities, questioning strategies, seating charts, pieces of content (e.g., text, pictures, and multimedia), and more for optimal student performance. Every decision is deliberate—from connecting standards (both content and processes) to learning objectives to knowledge of students to instructional strategies to activities (in that order). Nothing in this teacher's classroom is left to chance; he or she realizes that excellence is not an accident.

Alisa's Approach

Recently, I was explaining to my son how no two people have ever been found to have the same fingerprints—we are totally unique. As far as scientists can tell, there is a one in 64 billion chance that his fingerprints will match someone else's. We did some research and found that fingerprints are even more unique than DNA. And get this: although identical twins can share the same DNA, they can't have the same set of fingerprints (Komarinski, 2005). Fascinating thoughts.

This got me thinking. I've been an educator for more than 18 years now. I've taught in three different states and in multiple school districts, and I've spent time in hundreds of classrooms across the country. In my experiences and travels, I've never come across two classrooms that are exactly the same. Sure, some may share similar characteristics; they might even look the same. But no two are exactly alike. Each teacher creates a culture with the particular group of students that is unique to that classroom in that year. It's a culture that evolves and revolves around synergy—the interactions between teacher and students. At the heart of that unique, one-of-a-kind synergy is the teacher. It's an extraordinary thought, really.

I've been in many, many classrooms that were realizing tremendous academic achievements. They'd fit the definition of "excellence in education" quite aptly, yet none of them is the same as any of the others!

> There is no foolproof model for excellence, no formula for greatness. It is the teacher's exquisite uniqueness that helps facilitate deep learning—and that's the art of it all. Highly reflective teachers are, indeed, artists.

Ability to Accurately Assess: How do I know whether my actions affect student learning? In the Refinement stage, assessment does not signal the end of instruction. Every planned task, engagement activity, and "doing" in the classroom is considered an assessment, all of which provide the teacher with continuous information that will direct his or her next steps. This teacher has mastered the art of observation and strives to look beyond answers to analyze thinking. He or she knows students are successful when their self-assessment matches his or her evaluation of their learning. At all times, the teacher is watching, observing, listening, and seeing what's going on in the classroom. Because all decisions are intentional, he or she is observant of how students respond, whether his or her actions are yielding the intended outcomes, and why (or why not).

Capability to Adjust Actions: How effectively do I respond to the results of ongoing assessments? Data analysis is meaningless if it does not result in meaningful instructional change. The Refinement-stage teacher makes immediate, fluid adjustments to a lesson, responding directly to student questions, struggles, thinking, and actions. His or her responsiveness builds on what the student knows and addresses a specific need. For example, Sophie's exit ticket from one morning's math class is confusing and shows no understanding. Her Refinement-stage teacher knows that she needs more details before responding, so she pulls Sophie aside when she returns from lunch and asks her to explain her thinking. During the short exchange, the teacher realizes that Sophie is still struggling with conceptual understanding of 1:1 correspondence. Therefore, she decides to pull Sophie into her intervention group that meets daily and makes a note to provide manipulatives for tomorrow's follow-up lesson.

Frequency of Reflection: How often do I reflect? In order to have their fingers on the pulse of the lesson, Refinement-stage teachers proceed through the reflective cycle (i.e., building awareness, taking intentional action, accurately assessing, and adjusting their work) within mere seconds, over and over, each day. Through constant practice, these processes move into the subconscious and become second nature. In short, Refinement-stage teachers are always reflecting.

Goal for the Refinement Stage

Our capacity-building goal for teachers in the Refinement stage is to encourage your long-term growth and continued reflection. Though there may be short-term, immediate learning goals that require specific strategies and in-the-moment action, success in a classroom requires vision of the long-range goals, eventual outcomes, and skills needed to navigate the entire path. As you continue to build your reflective skills and tendencies, we'd also encourage you to share your learning with others, participate in leadership opportunities, and support the development of your colleagues and others.

Pete's Perspective

I like to think of myself as a pretty well-rounded athlete. Over the years, I have participated in a number of athletic endeavors, including two types of races: sprints and marathons. Though they both have some overarching similarities (starting lines, adrenaline, timing clocks, end goals, competition, and the need for post-race ice packs), there are quite a few distinguishing characteristics between the two.

When I sprint 100 meters, every step and every second counts . . . immensely. From the starting gun through the initial acceleration, I'm giving it everything I've got. If I stumble, it's over. In a sprint, the distance is too short and the time frame is too narrow to make up ground.

In a marathon, however, my mind-set is different. Acceleration and a quick start aren't as important as sustaining a steady pace, maintaining endurance, and finishing strong. A stumble here and a water stop there won't impede my ability to complete (and compete) in a multi-hour, 26.2-mile run.

My methods of training for these races also differ. From the equipment I use to train to my workouts, hydration strategies, nutrition, and mental approach, the goal determines my actions. And don't even get me started about how I must adapt my training, equipment, clothing, and gear for different courses: hilly versus flat, paved versus trail, a hot sunny day versus the threat of thunderstorms. In the end, as I'm striving to become a Refinement-stage racer, I must be prepared for whatever I'm about to experience—including the twists and turns I might not see coming.

Growing Along the Continuum

Ernest Hemingway said it best: "We are all apprentices in a craft where no one ever becomes a master." To be a Refinement-stage teacher does not mean that you've arrived and can stop reflecting. Quite the contrary; it means you're in tip-top shape and ready to run a grueling race. And then another grueling race. And another. And each one is different, so it takes constant refinement and preparation. Your habits of reflection are locked in, and you're ready to deepen your thoughtfulness about your professional practice. Having clear objectives is a proven effective strategy for enhancing learning, so we've provided specific targets for each of the five key components of the reflective cycle. As you continue to build your capacity as a reflective practitioner, we ask that you consider the following points.

Bring All the Variables Together. Reflective practitioners understand the factors that influence their classrooms and student learning. They are able to bring all the knowledge about their students—their backgrounds, home lives, lives outside of school, learning styles, gaps, and misconceptions—together. Reflective-stage teachers' knowledge of content extends to a deeper understanding of which concepts and skills are central and which are secondary. They are able to make connections across disciplines and weave their experience of best pedagogical practices together into the force that drives deep, meaningful learning.

Move Beyond Strategy to Design. To move from strategy to design means that your plans reflect a bigger purpose and picture—you use strategy to achieve the design. Rather than wait for a student to fail, you plan proactive interventions and supports for those who struggle. You anticipate the confusion that students are likely to have and uncover misconceptions early. With experience comes the ability to accurately predict how a lesson will go so that it minimizes modifications that need to be made mid-stream in order to optimize learning.

Assess with a Purpose. "Assessment that does not lead to intelligent instructional decisions is pointless at best and destructive at worst" (Hall & Simeral, 2008. p. 98). As our ability to design lessons improves, so does our ability to assess more accurately. We move from assessments *of* learning to assessments *for* learning, and we include students in this subtle shift as they set goals *for* their learning and track their own progress. Teachers and students work together in this venture, partnering with great intentionality to maximize student success.

Trust Your Intuition. We tend to think of intuition as a magical phenomenon, arising from a mysterious source within us. Steve Jobs called it "more powerful than intellect" (Isaacson, 2011, p. 48). However, scientists tell us it's actually a form of unconscious reasoning that is rooted in the same foundation used to make snap decisions (Rule, 2014). Reflective practitioners can trust their intuition when they think they see an unplanned but teachable moment arise. They've engaged in the reflective cycle enough to innately know when to ride the wind of a student's interest or allow a student to work through a problem independently, without correction. By trusting intuition, we bring all the resources of our brain into action.

Make Reflection a Priority. Teaching is more than showing up each day, engaging in all of the work we've addressed so far. There is important inner work that must be done outside of the bell schedule, committee meetings, parent nights, and district professional development. Time must be set aside to process, ponder, reorganize our thoughts, attain clarity, and innovate. Reflection invokes a power inside each of us to expand on what really matters and clear our minds of the things that don't.

Where Do I Start?

Continuing to grow as a reflective practitioner is a lifelong pursuit. Recruiting others to join you in this endeavor is one of the challenges you'll face in the Refinement stage. As a person of influence, you have that responsibility, though it's important to remember the words of Stephen Covey, author of *The 7 Habits of Highly Effective People*: "Leadership is a choice, not a position" (Covey, 1990, para. 8). So grab a pen and a pad, your favorite laptop or tablet, or whatever your tool of choice is to record your ideas and to track your thoughts—the reflecting hour is upon us.

We've compiled a thorough collection of viable strategies designed to increase your reflective habits, including tackling your own self-directed learning, engaging in student-focused analysis, accessing your colleagues within a Professional Learning Community, working with your instructional coach, and partnering with an administrator. Some of the strategies urge you to take action, try something new, or step out of your comfort zone. Others insist that you critically evaluate your belief system. Many will prompt you with questions, challenges, or ideas you'll need to learn about, explain, discuss, or at least *think* about. You needn't attempt these strategies in order, nor should you strive to complete the entire array of tasks included herein. The tasks and reflective questions are labeled alphanumerically for easy reference. Remember: your objective here is to build experience and strengthen expertise through the development of deeper reflective habits. So, with that end in mind, let's get started!

Options for Self-Directed Learning. Reflection starts and ends with you. Here, we'd like you to think about your job, your teaching, your planning, your goals, your purpose, and your thinking. Try these tasks and consider the embedded reflective questions—and record your thoughts in your reflective journal (which you'll have prepared after Task A).

A. Begin a reflective journal. Many teachers choose something artsy or classy, though any notebook or note-taking app will do. Research supports the notion that recording your thoughts about a topic can deepen your understanding and perspective on that topic (Hiemstra, 2001; Kerka, 1996; Killion, 1999). In addition, the practice poses numerous health benefits (Pennebaker, 1997). For one week, take two minutes at the end of the school day to jot down one success from the day (a WOW!) and something that challenged or surprised you (a YIKES!). These should be quick anecdotes from the day. Just write the date and two short sentences. At the end of the week, glance back at your thoughts. What do you notice about your thinking? Continue to journal each day and reflect at the end of each week.

B. Consider the piles of books, journals, and articles that are doubtlessly sitting on your desk, nightstand, or dining room table. In each are discussions of multiple research-based best practices for raising student achievement, and each has its own merits and evidence to support its use. How do you select appropriate strategies? When considering the learning goals of a particular lesson or unit, how do you select instructional strategies to implement? Are there other strategies that might be more effective in meeting your students' varied learning needs? How might you expand your repertoire of skills by trying new strategies? Keep track of the different teaching methods you use, including their effectiveness—and be specific about which students are successful, which students struggle, what type of learning goals you're tackling, and why certain lessons are effective or not. How might you continue to refine this practice?

Options for Student-Focused Learning. Siegfried Engelmann, senior educational specialist at the University of Illinois, states, "If the children aren't learning, we're not teaching" (quoted in Clowes, 2009, p. 13). It's with this in mind that we begin to take a deeper look at our students, who are the very reason we do what we do each day. Why are they the way they are? Are they learning? What do you know about them? How can you better support them? These questions and more drive the following tasks and reflective questions.

Tasks:

A. Most likely, you are well versed in the process of analyzing student data from a variety of sources: quizzes, tests, assignments, projects, papers, and even the in-process formative assessments that are connected to observations and anecdotal notes. Select an assessment tool that your entire department or grade-level team administered. Invite the team to your classroom to analyze the results of the assessment together. Follow a simple protocol: predict the results, review the data, analyze your findings, and determine a plan of action (there are several wonderful protocols for examining student work in *Protocols for Professional Learning* [Easton, 2009] that we highly recommend). Provide your colleagues with reflective prompts and engage them in speculative and objective discussion. How were students successful? How were they struggling? Why might this be the case? What instructional moves might contribute to students' successes and struggles? How might we respond in the future? When were your students successful while other teachers' students struggled, and vice versa? What can you learn from this analysis? Press one another for details about the instructional paths you followed. As much as you will discover about your students, their learning, your teaching, and the details of the content, you'll also grow in your knowledge and appreciation of your colleagues' varied approaches. Everyone wins when we engage in this work together.

B. Select one student who did not master the most recent learning objectives. Go back and review the topics, instructional strategies you used, assignments, quizzes, projects, and curriculum. What types of mistakes is he or she making? What does the evidence tell you about what he or she might know in relation to the objective? Sit down and have a conversation, and perhaps ask the student to explain his or her thinking to you. What insights does he or she provide? Do you notice any trends or patterns in the student's thinking? How might you use that information in the future? What intervention strategies might you now attempt?

Additional Reflective Questions:

1. How do your students fare in relation to their peers in other classes? What details can you elicit from your colleagues about their methods of achieving success?

2. Which instructional tasks provide the best opportunities to elicit informal assessment of student thinking?

3. What types of teacher-driven questions lead students to explain their thinking?

4. How do errors show what students know?

5. Do I notice any patterns or trends in student thinking that need to be addressed?

6. When a particular student struggles, is the inaccuracy at a conceptual, application, or procedural level?

7. What scaffolds need to be in place in order to make this student successful?

Options for Collaborative Learning. Isolated practice is one of the contributing factors to the gap between what is generally known about good teaching and its actual implementation in classrooms (Bird & Little, 1986). Teaching is no longer a task that we undertake independently. Instead, we are all members of a Professional Learning Community, working collaboratively with our grade-level teams, content departments, or whatever configuration our schools embrace. In that spirit, we must embrace the notion that our growth is partly the responsibility of our colleagues, just as their growth lies partly on our shoulders. Consider the following tasks and reflective questions while working with your colleagues to enhance your reflective tendencies.

Tasks:

A. *Action research* is a fancy term that describes the process of trying an innovative strategy to address a common problem of practice or something else you're struggling with. With your grade level, department, or team, identify something you're having trouble solving. Perhaps it's work completion, engagement, proper use of vocabulary, or the synthesis of information in writing a cohesive thesis statement. Lead the pursuit of investigating a strategy (or multiple strategies) that might solve this problem of practice. As a team, commit to learning as much as you can, implementing your new learning intentionally, and reporting back after a specified amount of time. What did you discover? What strategies hold promise? Lead the team in a continued investigation of ways to refine your thinking, learning, and application of this strategy. When you have gathered some information and data, offer to share with other grade levels, content teams, administrators, or the entire staff.

B. What instructional strategies is your department or grade-level team focusing on? If a colleague has proposed a book study, an article review, or a video analysis of this strategy, hop on board.

Recruit some of your colleagues to join the investigation—the more the merrier, and your vocal and visible support will lend credibility to the venture. Together, select elements of the strategy to try in your classrooms, and then report back on your initial findings. Embrace that concept and learn together.

Additional Reflective Questions:

1. Which colleagues do you feel you know the best? Which do you feel you know the least?

2. How might you begin to build deeper relationships with those you know the least in your grade level or department?

3. How might you cultivate a stronger team culture within your grade level or department?

4. What role can you play in bringing your grade level or department together around student learning?

5. How do you influence the success of your colleagues' students, and how do they affect the learning of yours?

6. What innovative ideas have you considered to meet diverse student needs? How might you investigate them further?

Options for Working with Your Instructional Coach. If you're lucky, you have an instructional coach at your disposal. This coach, if trained in the Continuum of Self-Reflection and the associated coaching strategies from our previous book—*Building Teachers' Capacity for Success* (Hall & Simeral, 2008)—will have specific goals and methods for supporting your reflective growth. Your coach will be willing to partner with you to investigate innovative approaches, engage in research, and nudge you into opportunities that positively influence your colleagues. You can also take an active role in the teacher-coach partnership by pursuing some of the tasks and reflective questions that follow.

Tasks:

A. Most likely, your instructional coach has extensive experience and expertise. What a fantastic resource! Putting your knowledge and experiences side-by-side can be a formidable tool to expand your repertoire of skills. Together, sit down and discuss various approaches to meeting the needs of diverse learners. What strategies have you attempted, have you heard about, or do you want to learn that you can investigate in greater detail? How might you attempt an innovative approach in your classroom? Which students would benefit? How might you have to temper that enthusiasm to still meet the needs of students for whom this approach might not be beneficial? Brainstorm and strategize together, and then make plans to attempt one (or more) of those strategies. Debrief with your coach to discuss and refine your findings.

B. Your instructional coach will ask you if there's anything you need to be more successful. Be prepared with a couple of options. Perhaps the coach can coteach a lesson with you, helping to capitalize (in the moment) on every instructional opportunity that arises in your lesson. It can be powerful to have a second set of eyes. You might also ask the coach to model a specific instructional technique for you, allowing you to sit back and observe students closely during learning. Keep your eyes wide open during this opportunity. What moments does the coach capitalize on (or miss) that might be chances to enhance student learning? What interventions does the coach slide into the lesson on the fly? How might you incorporate similar structures into your planning and lesson delivery? Debrief with your coach after the lesson.

C. Analyze video of your teaching with your instructional coach. Though this might feel uncomfortable at first (we suggest you watch the video alone the first time, just to get through the awkwardness of it), having someone next to you expands the scope of what you're able to notice. If you have clear look-fors, keep those in mind to focus your observations further. What do you see? How do students respond to certain actions and teaching strategies? Can you pinpoint specific steps you took that led to student learning? Alternatively, can you cite specific actions that impeded student learning? Add this knowledge to your planning regimen.

Additional Reflective Questions:

1. What do you believe about how kids learn? What other theories are out there that you might investigate to broaden your knowledge base?

2. What is an instructional strategy you have mastered? How do you know if it's effective?

3. What is an instructional strategy you've heard about but haven't implemented in your classroom? What do you already know about this strategy?

4. What opportunities are available for you to take leadership roles in your school?

5. What opportunities are available for you to take leadership roles in your district?

6. How can your instructional coach be of support to you? List 8–10 ways.

7. What innovative ideas have you considered to meet diverse student needs? How might you investigate them further with your instructional coach?

Options for Partnering with Your Administrator. Every school has an administrator who has a unique opportunity to provide feedback, guidance, and support to the instructional staff. Your administrator, if trained in the Continuum of Self-Reflection and its associated approach to walkthroughs and tailored feedback from our previous book, will have specific goals and methods for supporting your reflective growth. While working with teachers in the Refinement stage, the administrator's feedback will be tailored to drive your continued reflection. With a mix of reflective prompts and challenges to engage in leadership, your administrator is demonstrating that he or she values your thinking and seeks to expand the scope of your influence. Knowing this, you can build a strong growth-oriented relationship with your administrator by tackling some of the tasks and reflective questions that follow.

Tasks:

A. Be proactive. Ask your administrator to visit your classroom and provide you with specific feedback regarding your practice. It helps if you have a particular request. For example, ask your administrator to note which students are answering questions aloud during class and which students never get a chance to do so. This provides a focus for the administrator's observations and limits the amount of variables that come into play. It also helps if your particular request connects with a schoolwide instructional focus, your content or grade-level team's action plan, or your individual goal.

B. Invite your administrator to read and respond to entries in your reflective journal. In this sense, the journal becomes an interactive journal. (You could also offer this option to your instructional coach or a colleague you trust and respect.) This will require a significant amount of trust, as you'll be opening your thoughts, feelings, and reflections for review and response. If you are comfortable with a little bit of vulnerability, this can be an amazing way to build your relationship and maintain an ongoing dialogue about what's most important—your teaching.

C. Volunteer to engage in more formal avenues as a leader in your building and in the profession. In the Refinement stage, your thoughtfulness, intentionality, and impact radar are always scanning for ways to improve. Whether it's joining a school improvement team, participating in an ad hoc committee, contributing to staff development sessions, or coauthoring an article about a promising practice, your input and influence diversify our collective thinking, lend expertise to the discussion, and provide an opportunity to spread your leadership wings. Talk to your administrator about ways to ensure that your influence extends beyond your classroom walls.

D. Administrators are always looking for ways to partner teachers together, both to build experience and to enhance the Professional Learning Community. In that vein, offer to open up your classroom to a colleague's visit. Suggest that you'd like to be involved any time your administrator is seeking to develop new partnerships within the building. Structured visits, clear look-fors, and dedicated time for debriefing and dialogue can enrich both participants' experiences, adding value on both ends. This goes for hosting a student teacher as well—the conversations and intentional planning for each lesson help to solidify the purpose behind every action you take. In addition, a peripheral and very important benefit is spreading your influence to other teachers (and preservice teachers), which serves to strengthen the profession further.

Additional Reflective Questions:

1. What leadership opportunities might you pursue as a teacher leader? Discuss with your administrator.

2. Would you consider hosting a student teacher? Mentoring a novice? Facilitating a book club? List the pros and cons of each. Which outweighs the other?

3. What lesson would you like your administrator to observe and provide feedback on? Why would you choose that lesson?

4. What benefits might result from sharing your reflective journal with your administrator? What problems might arise? When might you talk with your administrator to share your hopes and worries?

5. What does your administrator expect from you regarding lesson plans, instructional techniques, data collection, classroom management, and participation in grade-level or content department meetings? How do you know?

6. What experiences does your administrator have that might enrich your perspective about becoming more of a teacher leader? When will you set up a time to "talk shop" together?

Conclusion: The Six-Week Challenge

Having read this chapter and tackled some of the strategies listed herein will not, by itself, create an overwhelmingly aware, intentional, reflective educator out of you. However, now that you've embarked on this journey, you're well on your way toward that end.

Remember that your goal as a Refinement-stage teacher is to continue to refine your thinking and practice in order to meet every single child's learning needs. By doing so, you'll be establishing yourself as a constant, critical thinker who is opting to move into the Refinement stage of the Continuum of Self-Reflection rather than just renting space.

In the meantime, if the wealth of strategies listed in this chapter left you scratching your head and wondering which bite to chew off first, if you prefer a more structured guideline, or if you're feeling strong about your reflective growth and would like to "wrap it up," here is the six-week challenge:

Week 1: Start your reflective journal. In it, begin to track your WOW! and YIKES! moments. (Self-Directed Learning, Task A)

Week 2: Engage your grade-level or department team in a data-driven dialogue. Record your thinking about the process so you can refine it next time. (Student-Focused Learning, Task A)

Week 3: Join a colleague's book study or investigation into a particular teaching strategy. Add to the dialogue and invite others to join as well. (Collaborative Learning, Task B)

Week 4: Offer to join a committee, school improvement team, or other leadership venture in your building. The opportunities are endless. (Partnering with Your Administrator, Task B)

Week 5: Ask your instructional coach to engage in some research about innovative strategies to address student needs. Keep track of your investigations in your journal. (Working with Your Instructional Coach, Task A)

Week 6: Take a thoughtful walk through your reflective journal. How do your WOW! and YIKES! examples look different this week when compared to the beginning of this journey? Write your reflection down in your journal. If you feel compelled to do so, share your thoughts and feelings on our blog, found online at http://bycfs.edublogs.org/. There, you can read other teachers' posts, comment on one another's reflections, and engage in some robust dialogue.

Summary Reflections

As a bonus, here is an additional challenge. Go back and reread this chapter, and then answer the following reflective questions.

1. How has your awareness of your students grown?

2. How has your awareness of content grown?

3. How has your awareness of pedagogy grown?

4. To what degree are your lesson plans more intentional?

5. What impact do you believe you have on student learning?

6. How often do you assess student learning?

7. What strategies do you use to determine whether students learn the intended targets?

8. What actions do you take when you first notice students struggling?

9. How do you plan for these on-the-spot interventions?

10. How frequently are you engaging in self-reflective actions?

The answers to these questions should provide you with ample evidence that you are growing as a reflective practitioner. We commend you for your efforts and energy in this venture, and we encourage you to maintain the continuous push for improvement. Don't worry if you don't recognize the changes just yet. This is often a lengthy process that requires dedication, perseverance, and more than a little bit of good old-fashioned nose-to-the-grindstone labor!

If you'd like, feel free to attempt the various tasks outlined in this chapter multiple times. Ask yourself the reflective questions over and over. There's no such thing as too much of a good thing—the more you practice and strive for improvement, the more you'll grow and progress as a reflective practitioner, which is a great thing! Your continued growth will ensure that you remain in the Refinement stage of the Continuum of Self-Reflection, constantly refining and improving your craft.

As George Sheehan suggests: "The music of a marathon is a powerful strain, one of those tunes of glory. It asks us to forsake pleasures, to discipline the body, to find courage, to renew faith, and to become one's own person, utterly and completely."

Conclusion

"It is good to have an end to journey toward; but it is the journey that matters, in the end."

—Ernest Hemingway

Take a moment to reflect on your journey through this book. After confirming your career choice as a teacher, you learned about the connections between self-reflection and your effectiveness in the classroom. Taking the self-assessment guided you toward a specific stage on the Continuum of Self-Reflection, and you gained some important information about how—and how frequently and accurately—you tend to reflect about your professional work. This was a vital step in your quest to grow as a reflective practitioner and effective educator, and we commend you for taking it!

Then you turned your focus to the chapter that centered on your current reflective state of mind, where you collected a handful (or more) of strategies, approaches, and reflective prompts to spur your development in the art and skill of self-reflection. You are certainly engaging in one (or more) of those tasks vigorously, earnestly, and passionately, befitting your commitment to the profession and this process of growth. You have entered the reflective cycle and are now traveling this path within it.

So now, here you are. We'd like to close by sharing a story about a fellow teacher's travels. This teacher—we'll call her Michele—is a blend of many real-life teachers with whom we've worked over the years. Her story is realistic fiction, as the events actually did occur to a mix of teachers, but we've woven them together into one succinct narrative. As you read it, please know that our goal is to inspire you to continue along this path, even though it may seem circuitous, lengthy, overgrown, and full of challenging impediments. We also challenge you to apply your knowledge of the Continuum of Self-Reflection to identify the stages at which Michele operates and grows through during her very deliberate (and very repeatable) travels toward refined thinking.

Michele's Story

When Michele was first hired to teach 6th grade at Lakeview Heights Middle School, she was ecstatic. Calling her parents, she exclaimed, "I got it! I got the job! I'm going to be a teacher, and I'm going to change the world!"

Full of pep and energy, Michele spent countless hours in her classroom leading up to the first day of school, soaking up the smell of textbooks, the feel of the worn wooden-top desks, the sounds of the tetherball chain clanging against its pole on the playground, and the images of the 27 wonderful young people who would fill her classroom. She was prepared. She had worked hard to accomplish this goal, and now it was hers.

As the first day approached, her giddiness and excitement mixed with trepidation and uncertainty. What if the students didn't warm up to her? What if they failed? What if she failed? 'Nope,' she decided, 'I'm not going to go there. My students will learn everything they're supposed to learn and then some! It will be a fabulous year and an extraordinary career. Bring it on!'

Six years later, Michele sat at a table with three strangers—fellow teachers—in a hotel conference room at an education workshop in Boston. It was a sticky summer day outside, though the air conditioning in the conference center had many attendees wishing they had brought a sweatshirt. Shifting in her seat, Michele zoned out a little bit and began reflecting on her career. How did she get here?

When her teaching career began, Michele had high hopes and a ton of energy. Her first year was a blur, and she was hard-pressed to remember many of the details. As she recalled, the students were ruthless, the pacing guide she had to follow was relentless, and the amount of planning and grading she had to take home every day consumed most of her waking energy. Though she was open to her colleagues' expertise and her administrators' support, she had wanted to prove herself worthy, so she persevered without asking for much help. It was a long year, and by the second semester she was in full-blown survival mode. She just wanted to make it through to June.

During the next five years, not a whole lot had changed. Michele's enthusiasm for the school year began waning earlier and earlier until she found herself dreading coming to work every day. By the end of year six, she had admitted to herself that this wasn't going well, and she had requested a change of placement. Her new principal agreed, and Michele was now an 8th grade English and Social Studies teacher.

At the two-day conference in Boston, she and a couple hundred other educators from around the country were learning about various topics. Michele had chosen to attend sessions in which she'd learn the new English standards, engage in some curriculum mapping, and get an overview of the relationship between self-reflection and teacher effectiveness. She sighed. A six-year veteran teacher should not be facing this sort of steep learning curve. But here she was. She needed to do things differently, and she was ready for the change.

Taking That First Leap

By the end of the conference, the butterflies had returned to Michele's stomach. But this time, they were reminiscent of the giddy enthusiasm she felt as she first embarked on her dream career. The workshop on self-reflection had truly opened her eyes to the reality of her situation. She had spent so much of her energy on surviving each day that she hadn't ever stopped to take stock of her reality. She was so focused on her struggles that she hadn't acknowledged her own strengths. And she was so consumed by the day-to-day grind that she had never really taken charge of her teaching, her career, or her life! That, she decided, was about to change.

When she returned home, Michele immediately called her best friend and fellow teacher, Mark. They sipped lemonade and discussed the state of education, the barrage of requirements coming at them, and the challenges they faced. And then, Michele turned her critical eye inward.

"Mark," she said, "I've been thinking. Truly thinking. For the first time in my career, I have a realistic plan." She proceeded to share the ideas she garnered from the Boston workshop and that she'd refined during her flight home. She would become the master of her own destiny as a teacher. This called for a daily moment of reflection—a time in which she would wall off the world and think, both deeply and critically, about her teaching, her students, the content, and the progress they're making together toward learning it.

She asked Mark if he'd be willing to meet with her once a week to go through lesson plans, analyze student work, and discuss items that needed discussing. "I've already gotten our instructional coach, Sienna, to agree to meet with me—and you, if you want to—once a week, too. There are a couple of strategies for engaging students, increasing our focus on writing, and using formative assessments that I'd like to put into place. Our kids are going to learn this year, Mark. There's no getting around it. Enough is enough." They clinked glasses and proceeded to chat.

By February, Michele was furiously attempting to ward off her frustrations. Her meetings with Mark were hit-and-miss, based on their schedules and competing demands. Sienna, the instructional coach, was similarly busy but still managed to join Michele's scheduled meetings. The demands of the new standards, the pressure from the new teacher-evaluation system, and the learning struggles presented by her students caused Michele a significant amount of grief.

"I've bitten off more than I can chew, haven't I?" Michele asked Sienna.

"What makes you say that?" Sienna returned.

"Because I am having trouble keeping my head above water." Michele's intended focus of engagement, writing, and assessments had disintegrated into a battle for classroom management, lackluster lessons, and only the occasional formative gauges of student progress.

She looked at Sienna pleadingly. "What should I do?"

"You've got a knowing-doing gap," Sienna shared. "You're smart, you've learned a lot, you have some amazing experiences, and you're having trouble implementing what you know with consistency and intentionality."

Michele frowned. "How do I fix this?"

"Let's start," Sienna smiled, "by biting off something you *can* chew. Let's pick one goal, not three, and let's set a short-term goal you can accomplish with success."

Taking Action

Together, Michele and Sienna contemplated their options and agreed that focusing on increasing student-engagement rates would have many residual benefits, including reduced management issues, heightened learning, and a more enjoyable classroom experience for everyone involved. So they got to work.

Right off the bat, Michele began to implement some of the engagement strategies she had learned months ago in Boston. She added to this strategy by surveying the students to determine which of the new strategies they preferred to accept as part of their classroom routines. She also collected data from lessons in which she used different strategies and analyzed them with Sienna and Mark, noting which strategies tended to yield greater returns. These strategies became part of her staple plans.

By the start of the following school year, Michele and her teammates had created a bank of strategies that worked—they kept the students' attention, involved the students in learning activities, and resulted in higher rates of achievement. With Sienna's support, Michele and Mark continued to monitor the effectiveness of their strategies, adding instructional techniques, assessment tools, and motivational incentives to their list of "things that work."

Michele's new routine became the reflective cycle. What once was a cursory step she took at the beginning of each semester when she received a new set of class rosters became part of her modus operandi: Gain a comprehensive understanding of her students and courses, create intentional plans to lead her students toward the learning goals, assess the impact of various strategies on learning, adapt the strategies immediately if they aren't working, and constantly keep her eyes and ears open for ways to refine the goings-on in her classroom.

It was at the end of her tenth year that she found herself, once again, on the phone with her parents. "I got it!" she exclaimed. "I got it! My kids rocked it again this year, and I won the district's Teacher of the Year award! It's finally happening; I'm changing the world."

Final Words

We're educators. That goes for the small, specific *we* (the authors) and the whole, general *we* (the readers, teachers, leaders, and education professionals). In our scenario, Michele won a fancy award, but we're not in this business for accolades and recognition. We're not in it for the money, either, and there's a black eye waiting for the next person who claims we're in it for summer vacations.

No, we're in the education business because we want to change the world, just like Michele. We want to make a difference—one child, class, day, school, and year at a time. We have a vision of a brighter, better future, and we know that working with youth is the way to realize it. We are members of the most noble, meaningful, important, service-oriented profession that exists.

Every child matters. Every second counts. There's a certain degree of urgency behind our work, yes, but it doesn't stem from newspaper articles, district offices, laws, the Twitter feed. Rather, our urgency comes from the constant marching of time. As the seconds pass, our students get older and the time they have remaining in school—the time they have remaining with us—rapidly decreases. We must capitalize on every precious moment if we're to convert today's visions and dreams into tomorrow's reality.

We commend you for tackling the challenge. We thank you for committing to this work with your heart, soul, and reflective mind. And we'd like to inspire you to continue down the path. All of us, together, can move mountains. Think about it.

●●●●●●●

When you feel comfortable that you've made it through the book, you've engaged in some intentional strategies, and you've made some growth as a reflective practitioner, go back and retake the self-assessment in Chapter 3. If the results are the same, keep plugging away, this time using different strategies. If the results are different, go to the relevant chapter and get to work. There's no time to wait!

Appendix A
Self-Assessment Chart

For those of you who have completed the self-assessment tool and would like to drill down into the questions, the following chart illustrates which of the five components of reflection each question addresses. You might ask yourself: Which area was a clear strength of mine? Is there an area that returned a lower score? Do these scores seem accurate to you? What might have contributed to some of your responses? As you reflect further, do your responses change? Why or why not?

Questions that address Awareness of Instructional Reality

Q7: When describing the students I teach each day, I . . .	My score:
Q10: When reflecting on my students' assessment performance levels, I . . .	My score:

Questions that address Intentionality of Actions

Q1: When planning for today's (or tomorrow's) lesson, I . . .	My score:
Q3: When planning to address student misconceptions, I . . .	My score:
Q6: When I ask questions in class, I . . .	My score:

Questions that address Ability to Accurately Assess

Q4: When I encounter students who struggle in a lesson, I . . .	My score:
Q9: When determining the level of success in a particular unit, I . . .	My score:

Questions that address Capability to Adjust Actions

Q5: When attempting to reengage students who are off-task, I . . .	My score:
Q8: When students are struggling in a lesson, I . . .	My score:

Question that addresses Frequency of Reflection

Q2: When considering the frequency that I reflect on my teaching, I . . .	My score:

Appendix B
Reflective Cycle Goal Chart

	Unaware	Conscious	Action	Refinement
REFLECTIVE CYCLE GOALS:	◆ OBSERVE ◆ THINK INTENTIONALLY ◆ NOTICE LEARNING ◆ MAKE CHANGES ◆ PRACTICE REFLECTION	◆ NOTE CAUSE/EFFECT RELATIONSHIPS ◆ PLAN WITH INTENTIONALITY ◆ RECOGNIZE THE RESULTS OF YOUR ACTIONS ◆ RESPOND TO THE NEEDS YOU SEE ◆ COMMIT TO REFLECTING EACH DAY	◆ ZOOM IN ON THE DETAILS ◆ STRATEGIZE ◆ CONSIDER STUDENT THINKING AS YOU ASSESS ◆ RESPOND IN THE MOMENT ◆ DEVELOP A PATTERN OF REFLECTION	◆ BRING ALL THE VARIABLES TOGETHER ◆ MOVE BEYOND STRATEGY TO DESIGN ◆ ASSESS WITH A PURPOSE ◆ TRUST YOUR INTUITION ◆ CULTIVATE REFLEXIVE REFLECTION
Self	▪ Reflective Journal ▪ Reflective Wow/Yikes	▪ Reflective Journal with Wow/Yikes ▪ Closer look at habits ▪ Reflect on obstacles to following through ▪ Set a goal	▪ Reflective Journal with Wow/Yikes ▪ Lesson to examine closely ▪ Belief how students learn	▪ Reflective Journal with Wow/Yikes ▪ Research best practices
Student	▪ Class list of interests ▪ Student needs to know more about. . . . ▪ Student to become an expert on. . . .	▪ Student to become an expert on . . . ▪ Change questioning strategy and note response to change ▪ Assumptions you have of students	▪ Student to become an expert on . . . ▪ Analyze student mistakes ▪ Coach teaches lesson so you can watch students	▪ Lead a team with data-driven dialogue ▪ Analyze student mistakes

Collaborative	▪ Think about the content you are teaching ▪ Visit colleague's class ▪ Play Give One Get One	▪ Ask colleagues "What does reflection look like to you?" ▪ Ask a colleague to help plan a lesson ▪ Analyze student work with colleague ▪ Participate in book study	▪ Visit colleague's class ▪ Analyze student work with colleague ▪ Spearhead a book study	▪ Join a colleague's book study ▪ Establish a team action research project
Coach	▪ Coach teaches lesson ▪ Coach covers your class-you observe colleague ▪ Coach examines admin feedback	▪ Coach teaches lesson ▪ Develop detailed action plan with coach ▪ Coach examines admin feedback	▪ Develop partnership with coach ▪ Coach covers your class-you observe colleague ▪ Coach examines admin feedback ▪ Analyze video of your teaching	▪ Discuss innovative strategies and approaches ▪ Coach teaches lesson – you analyze students ▪ Analyze video of your teaching
Administrator	▪ Admin visits classroom and provides feedback ▪ Interactive reflective journal ▪ Ask clarifying questions with admin & coach	▪ Request regular admin visits with feedback ▪ Ask clarifying questions with admin & coach ▪ Set short term goal with admin	▪ Request admin visit & feedback ▪ Interactive reflective journal ▪ Ask clarifying questions with admin & coach ▪ Request opportunities to extend learning (conference, journal)	▪ Request admin visit & feedback ▪ Interactive reflective journal ▪ Volunteer to be a teacher leader in your building ▪ Offer to host colleagues' visits and student teachers

•••••••

Appendix C
Quick-Win Goal-Setting Form

Selecting and working toward an area of professional growth is an admirable path to choose. As you travel this course, record your thoughts, feelings, observations, and questions regularly in your reflective journal. Review them often and include a trusted colleague, coach, or administrator in the conversation.

What is an area of focus you'd like to address?

Rewrite this focus as a goal statement. What would you like to accomplish?

Identify a timeline for accomplishing this goal. (We suggest no more than a four-week window, with weekly check-ins.) Write the specific dates below:

Accomplish Date:

Check-in #1:

Check-in #2:

Check-in #3:

Check-in #4:

Record three action steps that you will commit to implementing—intentionally and consistently—in order to achieve this goal. Use colleagues, coaches, and administrators to help you create this plan.

Action Step A:

Action Step B:

Action Step C:

Who will serve as your accountability partner, ensuring your consistent and intentional follow-through with these action steps, check-in dates, and perseverance toward your goal? Why did you select this person?

How will you celebrate your accomplishment and progress toward the goal?

Bibliography

Ainsworth, L., & Viegut, D. (2006). *Common formative assessments.* Thousand Oaks, CA: Corwin.

Allington, R., & Cunningham, P. (2007). *Schools that work: Where all children read and write* (3rd ed.). Boston: Allyn & Bacon.

Allington, R., & Walmsley, S. (1995). *No quick fix: Rethinking literacy programs in America's elementary schools.* New York: Teachers College Press.

Amabile, T., & Kramer, S. (2010). What really motivates workers: Understanding the power of progress. *Harvard Business Review, 88*(1), 44–45.

Anderson, L.W., Krathwohl, D. R., Airasian, P. W., Cruikshank, K. A., Mayer, R. E., Pintrich, P. R., et al. (Eds.). (2001). *A taxonomy for learning, teaching, and assessing: A revision of Bloom's taxonomy of educational objectives.* New York: Longman.

Angelo T. A., & Cross, K. P. (1993). *Classroom assessment techniques: A handbook for college teachers* (2nd ed.). San Francisco: Jossey-Bass.

Archambault, R. D. (Ed.). (1974). *John Dewey on education: Selected writings.* Chicago: Chicago University Press.

Atherton, J. S. (2005). Learning and teaching: Reflection and reflective practice. Retrieved from: http://www.learningandteaching.info/learning/reflecti .htm

Aubrey, A. (2013). Whole milk or skim? Study links fattier milk to slimmer kids. Retrieved from: http://www.npr.org/blogs/thesalt/2013/03/19/174739752/ whole-milk-or-skim-study-links-fattier-milk-to-slimmer-kids

Aubrey, A. (2014). The full-fat paradox: Whole milk may keep us lean. Retrieved from: http://www.npr.org/blogs/thesalt/2014/02/12/275376259/the -full-fat-paradox-whole-milk-may-keep-us-lean

Ball, S. J. (1987). *The micro-politics of the school: Towards a theory of school organization.* London: Methuen.

Bandura, A. (1977). *Social learning theory.* Englewood Cliffs, NJ: Prentice Hall.

Barr, A. S. (1958). Characteristics of successful teachers. *Phi Delta Kappan, 39,* 282–284.

Barth, R. (1990). *Improving schools from within: Teachers, parents, and principals can make the difference.* San Francisco: Jossey-Bass.

Bellanca, J., & Fogarty, J. (1986). *Catch them thinking.* Kankakee, IL: Imperial International Learning Corporation.

Ben-Hur, M. (2006). *Concept-rich math instruction: Building a strong foundation for reasoning and problem-solving.* Alexandria, VA: ASCD.

Bender, W., & Shores, C. (2007). *Response to intervention: A practical guide for every teacher.* Thousand Oaks, CA: Corwin.

Bird, T., & Little, J. W. (1986). How schools organize the teaching occupation. *Elementary School Journal, 86*(4), 493–511.

Black, P., & William, D. (1998). Assessment and classroom learning. *Assessment in Education, 5*(1), 7–75.

Bloom, B., Engelhart, M., Furst, E., Hill, W., & Krathwohl, D. (1956). *Taxonomy of educational objectives: The classification of educational goals.* Handbook I: Cognitive domain. New York: David McKay Company.

Bolman, L. G., & Deal, T. E. (2001). *Leading with soul: An uncommon journey of spirit.* San Francisco: Jossey-Bass.

Boud, D., Keogh, R., & Walker, D. (1985). *Reflection: Turning experience into learning.* London: Kogan Page.

Brookfield, S. D. (1995). *Becoming a critically reflective teacher.* San Francisco: Jossey-Bass.

Bryk, A., & Schneider, B. (2004). *Trust in schools: A core resource for improvement.* New York: Russell Sage.

Buchmann, M. (1990). Beyond the lonely, choosing will: Professional development in teacher thinking. *Teachers College Record, 91*(4), 481–508.

Buffum, A., Mattos, M., & Weber, C. (2010). The why behind RTI. *Educational Leadership, 68*(2), 10–16.

California Department of Education. (2008). Closing the achievement gap: "You know what to do, teachers. Now do it." *The Special Edge, 21*(2). Retrieved from: http://www.calstat.org/publications/spedge_publications.php?nl_id=12

Carroll, T., Fulton, K., & Doerr, H. (2010). *Team up for 21st century teaching and learning: What research and practice reveal about professional learning.* Washington, DC: National Commission on Teaching and America's Future.

Centers for Disease Control and Prevention. (2014). FastStats: Heart disease data are for the U.S. Retrieved from: http://www.cdc.gov/nchs/fastats/heart-disease.htm

Chenoweth, K. (2009). It can be done, it's being done, and here's how. *Phi Delta Kappan, 91*(1), 38–43.

Chetty, R., Friedman, J., & Rockoff, J. (2011). *The long-term impacts of teachers: Teacher value-added and student outcomes in adulthood.* Cambridge, MA: National Bureau of Economic Research.

Chicago Project on Learning and Teaching. (1992). *Best practice: Teaching and learning in Chicago.* Chicago: Chicago Project on Learning and Teaching, National-Louis University.

Clowes, G. (2009). "If the children aren't learning, we're not teaching": An interview with Siegfried E. Engelmann. *The Utah Special Educator, 32*(2): 13–15. Retrieved from: http://www.updc.org/assets/files/utah_special_educator/pdfs/dec2009-academics.pdf

Cole, R. W. (Ed.) (1995). *Educating everybody's children: Diverse teaching strategies for diverse learners.* Alexandria, VA: ASCD.

Cole, R. W., & Schlechty, P. C. (1992). Teachers as trailblazers. *Educational Horizons, 70*(3), 135–137.

Coleman, J. S. (1966). Equality of educational opportunity (COLEMAN) study (EEOS).

Common Core State Standards Initiative. (2010). *Common core state standards for English language arts & literacy in history/social studies, science, and technical subjects.* Washington DC: National Governors Association Center for Best Practices and Council of Chief State School Officers.

Cone, J. K. (1992). Untracking advanced placement English: Creating opportunity is not enough. *Phi Delta Kappan, 73*(9), 712–717.

Covey, S. (1990). *The 7 habits of highly effective people: Powerful lessons in personal change.* New York: Simon & Schuster.

Covey, S. (2009). Leadership is a choice, not a position. *Business Standard.* Retrieved from: http://www.business-standard.com/article/management/leadership-is-a-choice-not-a-position-stephen-r-covey-109020300076_1.html

Cross, K. P. (2001). Leading-edge efforts to improve teaching and learning: The Hesburgh Awards. *Change, 33*(4), 30–37.

Danielson, C. (2007). *Enhancing professional practice: A framework for teaching* (2nd ed.). Alexandria, VA: ASCD.

Danielson, C., & McGreal, T. (2000). *Teacher evaluation to enhance professional practice.* Alexandria, VA: ASCD.

Darling-Hammond, L. (1990). Instructional policy into practice: "The power of the bottom over the top." *Educational Evaluation and Policy Analysis, 12*(3), 339–347.

Darling-Hammond, L., & McLaughlin, M. (1995). Policies that support professional development in an era of reform. *Phi Delta Kappan, 76*(8), 597–604.

Daudelin, M. W. (199). Learning from experience through reflection. *Organizational Dynamics, 24*(3), 36–48.

Daudelin, M. W., & Hall, D. T. (1997). Using reflection to leverage learning. *Training and Development, 51*(12), 13–14.

Desimone, L., Porter, A., Garet, M., Yoon, K., & Birman, B. (2002). Effects of professional development on teachers' instruction: Results from a three-year longitudinal study. *Educational Evaluation and Policy Analysis, 24*(2), 81–112.

Dethy, F. (2009). Medical students learn 'art' of observation. *Yale Daily News.* Retrieved from: http://yaledailynews.com/blog/2009/04/22/medical-students-learn-art-of-observation

Dewey, J. (1910). *How we think.* New York: Heath and Company.

Dewey, J. (1933). *How we think: A restatement of the relation of reflective thinking to the education process.* Lexington, MA: Heath and Company.

Duffett, A., Farkas, S., Rotherham, A. J., & Silva, E. (2008). *Waiting to be won over: Teachers speak on the profession, unions, and reform.* Washington, DC: Educational Sector.

DuFour, R., & Eaker, R. (1998). *Professional learning communities at work: Best practices for enhancing student achievement.* Bloomington, IN: National Educational Service.

DuFour, R., & Marzano, R. (2011). *Leaders of learning: How district, school, and classroom leaders improve student achievement.* Bloomington, IN: Solution Tree.

Duhigg, C. (2012). *The power of habit: Why we do what we do in life and business.* New York: Random House.

Dweck, C. (2006). *Mindset: The new psychology of success.* New York: Ballantine.

Easton, L. (2009). *Protocols for professional learning.* Alexandria, VA: ASCD.

Elder, L., & Paul, R. (2009). *Guide to critical thinking.* Dillon Beach, CA: Foundation for Critical Thinking.

Ellwood, C. (1992). *Teacher research for whom?* Paper presented at the annual meeting of the American Educational Research Association, San Francisco.

Erwin, J. C. (2004). *The classroom of choice: Giving students what they need and getting what you want.* Alexandria, VA: ASCD.

Evans, R. (2001). *The human side of school change: Reform, resistance and the real-life problems of innovation.* San Francisco: Jossey-Bass.

Evertson, C. M., & Murphy, J. (1992). Beginning with the classroom: Implications for redesigning schools. In H. H. Marshall (Ed.), *Redefining student learning: Roots of educational change* (pp. 283–320). Norwood, NJ: Ablex.

Fine, M. (in press). *Restructuring in the midst.* New York: Teachers College Press.

Fisher, D., & Frey, N. (2007). *Checking for understanding: Formative assessment techniques for your classroom.* Alexandria, VA: ASCD.

Fiske, E. (1992). *Smart schools, smart kids: Why do some schools work?* New York: Simon & Schuster.

Flinders, D. J. (1988). Teacher isolation and the new reform. *Journal of Curriculum and Supervision, 4*(1), 17–29.

Freire, P. (1970). *Pedagogy of the oppressed.* New York: Continuum.

Fullan, M. (1991). *The new meaning of educational change.* New York: Teachers College Press.

Fullan, M. (2010). *Motion leadership: The skinny on becoming change savvy.* Thousand Oaks, CA: Corwin.

Garmston, R., & Wellman, B. (1999). *The adaptive school: A source-book for developing collaborative groups.* Norwood, MA: Christopher-Gordon.

Gladwell, M. (2007). *Blink: The power of thinking without thinking.* New York: Little, Brown.

Gleick, J. (1998). *Chaos: Making a new science.* New York: Penguin.

Goddard, R. D., Hoy, W. K., & Hoy, A. W. (2000). Collective teacher efficacy: Its meaning, measure, and impact on student achievement. *American Educational Research Journal, 37*(2), 479–507.

Goddard, R. D., Hoy, W. K., & Hoy, A. W. (2004). Collective efficacy beliefs: Theoretical developments, empirical evidence, and future directions. *Educational Researcher, 33*(3), 3–13.

Goodlad, J. (1984). *A place called school: Prospects for the future.* New York: McGraw-Hill.

Goodwin, B., & Hubbell, E. R. (2013). *The 12 touchstones of good teaching: A checklist for staying focused every day.* Alexandria, VA: ASCD.

Greenleaf, R. (1970). *The servant as leader.* Indianapolis, IN: Robert K. Greenleaf Center for Servant-Leadership.

Guskey, T. R. (1986). Staff development and the process of teacher change. *Educational Researcher. 15*(5), 5–12.

Guskey, T. R. (2009). *The teacher as assessment leader.* Bloomington, IN: Solution Tree.

Hall, P. (2005). A school reclaims itself. *Educational Leadership, 62*(5), 70–73.

Hall, P., & Simeral, A. (2008). *Building teachers' capacity for success: A collaborative approach for coaches and school leaders.* Alexandria, VA: ASCD.

Hanushek, E. (2011). The economic value of higher teacher quality. *Economics of Education Review, 30*(2011) 466–479.

Hargreaves, A. (1990). Teachers' work and the politics of time and space. *Qualitative Studies in Education, 3*(4), 303–320.

Hargreaves, A. (1992). Time and teachers' work: Teacher preparation time and the intensification thesis. *Teachers College Record, 94*(1), 87–108.

Hargreaves, A. (1993). Individualism and individuality: Reinterpreting the teacher culture. In J. W. Little and M. W. McLaughlin, *Teachers' work: Individuals, colleagues, and contexts* (pp. 51–76). New York: Teachers College Press.

Hargreaves, A., & Dawe, R. (1990). Paths of professional development: Contrived collegiality, collaborative culture, and the case of peer coaching. *Teaching and Teacher Education, 6*(3), 227–241.

Hattie, J. (2009). *Visible learning: A synthesis of over 800 meta-analyses relating to student achievement.* New York: Routledge.

Haycock, K. (1998). Good teaching matters . . . a lot. *Thinking K–16, 3*(2), 1–14.

Heacox, D. (2012). *Differentiating instruction in the regular classroom: How to reach and teach all learners.* Minneapolis, MN: Free Spirit.

Hiemstra, R. (2001). Uses and benefits of journal writing. *New directions for adult and continuing education, 90,* 19–26.

Holmberg, S., & Thelin, A. (2013). High dairy fat intake related to less central obesity: A male cohort study with 12 years' follow-up. *Scandinavian Journal of Primary Health Care, 31*(2): 89–94.

International Health, Racquet & Sportsclub Association. (2014). *U.S. health club membership exceeds 50 million.* Retrieved from: http://www.ihrsa.org/news/2011/4/5/us-health-club-membership-exceeds-50-million-up-108-industry.html

Isaacson, W. (2011.) *Steve Jobs.* New York: Simon & Schuster.

Joyce, B., Murphy, C., Showers, B., & Murphy, J. (1989). School renewal as cultural change. *Educational Leadership, 47*(3), 70–77.

Kerka, S. (1996). Journal writing and adult learning. *ERIC Digest No. 174.* Retrieved from: www.ericdigests.org/1997-2/journal.htm

Killion, J. (1999). Journaling. *National Staff Development Council.* Retrieved from: http://epfarms.org/~fbarton/files/reflection/killion203.pdf

Kise, J. (2006). *Differentiated coaching: A framework for helping teachers change.* Thousand Oaks, CA: Sage.

Komarinski, P. (2005). *Automated fingerprint identification systems* (AFIS). Waltham, MA: Academic Press.

Kratz, M., Baars, T., & Guyenet, S. (2013). The relationship between high-fat dairy consumption and obesity, cardiovascular, and metabolic disease. *European Journal of Nutrition, 52*(1): 1–24.

Lorenz, E. N. (1963). Deterministic Nonperiodic Flow. *Journal of the Atmospheric Sciences, 20*(2): 130–141.

Martinez, A. R. (2010). The improvisational brain. *Seed Magazine.* Retrieved from: http://seedmagazine.com/content/article/the_improvisational_brain/P1/

Marzano, R. (2007). *The art and science of teaching.* Alexandria, VA: ASCD.

Marzano, R., Pickering, D., & Pollock, J. (2001). *Classroom instruction that works: Research-based strategies for increasing student achievement.* Alexandria, VA: ASCD.

McTighe, J., & Wiggins, G. (2004). *Understanding by design.* Alexandria, VA: ASCD.

Meier, D. (1992). Reinventing teaching. *Teachers College Record, 93*(4), 594–609.

Miller, C., & Saxton, J. (2004). *Into the story: Language in action through drama.* Portsmouth, NH: Heinemann.

Moon, J. (1999). *Reflection in learning and professional development.* London: Kogan Page.

Muniz, K. (2014, March 24). 20 ways Americans are blowing their money. *USA Today.* Retrieved from: www.usatoday.com/story/money/personalfinance /2014/03/24/20-ways-we-blow-our-money/6826633/

Murphy, J. (1991). *Restructuring schools: Capturing and assessing the phenomena.* New York: Teachers College Press.

Murphy, P. K. & Alexander, P. A. (2006). *Understanding how students learn: A guide for instructional leaders.* Thousand Oaks, CA: Corwin.

National Board for Professional Teaching Standards. (2002). *What teachers should know and be able to do.* Arlington, VA: NBPTS.

National Board for Professional Teaching Standards. (2012). The five core propositions. Retrieved from: http://www.nbpts.org/five-core-propositions

Newmann, F. M., Secada, W. G., & Wehlage, G. C. (1995). *A guide to authentic instruction and assessment: Vision, standards and scoring.* Madison, WI: Wisconsin Center for Educational Research.

Oakes, J. (1992). Can tracking research inform practice? Technical, normative, and political considerations. *Educational Researcher, 21*(4), 12–21.

Peale, N. V. (1976). *The positive principle today.* New York: Random House.

Pennebaker, J. (1997). *Opening up: The healing power of expressing emotions.* New York: Guilford.

Peterson, P. (1992). Doing more in the same amount of time: Cathy Swift. *Educational Evaluation and Policy Analysis, 12*(3), 261–280.

Pfeffer, J., & Sutton, R. (2000). *The knowing-doing gap: How smart companies turn knowledge into action.* Boston: President and Fellows of Harvard College.

Pink, D. (2009). *Drive: The surprising truth about what motivates us.* New York: Riverhead.

Reeves, D. B. (2004). *Making standards work: How to implement standards-based assessment in the classroom, school, and district.* Englewood, CO: Advanced Learning Press.

Reeves, D. B. (2009). *Leading change in your school: How to conquer myths, build commitment, and get results.* Alexandria, VA: ASCD.

Rule, N. O. (2014). Snap-judgment science: Intuitive decisions about other people. *Association for Psychological Science.* Retrieved from: www
.psychologicalscience.org/index.php/publications/observer/2014/may
-june-14/snap-judgment-science.html

Ryan, R. M., & Deci, E. L. (2000). Self-determination theory and the facilitation of intrinsic motivation, social development, and well-being. *American Psychologist, 55*(1), 68–78.

Shallwani, P. (2009). A shift to recipe-less cooking. *The Wall Street Journal.* Retrieved from: http://online.wsj.com/articles/SB123808950657349873

Shon, D. (1983). *The reflective practitioner: How professionals think in action.* New York: Basic Books.

Sinek, S. (2009). How great leaders inspire action. Retrieved from: http://www
.ted.com/talks/simon_sinek_how_great_leaders_inspire_action

Sinek, S. (2011). *Start with why: How great leaders inspire everyone to take action.* New York: Penguin.

Sizer, T. (1992). *Horace's school: Redesigning the American high school.* Boston: Houghton Mifflin.

Statistics Brain. (2014). *New Year's Resolution Statistics.* Retrieved from: www
.statisticbrain.com/new-years-resolution-statistics/

Strong, R. W., Silver, H. F., & Perini, M. J. (2001). *Teaching what matters most: Standards and strategies for raising student achievement.* Alexandria, VA: ASCD.

Toffler, A. (1970). *Future shock.* New York: Random House.

Tomlinson, C. (2014). *The differentiated classroom: Responding to the needs of all learners (2nd ed.)*. Alexandria, VA: ASCD.

U.S. National Commission on Excellence in Education. (1983). A nation at risk: The imperative for educational reform: A report to the nation and the secretary of education, United States Department of Education (Vol. 2). Ann Arbor, MI: University of Michigan Library.

Wagner, J. (1991). *Teacher professionalism and school improvement in an occupational community of teachers of English*. Paper presented at the Ethnography and Education Forum, University of Pennsylvania, Philadelphia, PA.

Walk, H. (2013). The growing knowing<>doing gap. Retrieved from: https://www.linkedin.com/pulse/20130111155642-7298-the-growing-knowing-doing-gap

Vygotsky, L. (1978). *Mind in society: The development of higher psychological processes*. Cambridge, MA: Harvard University Press.

Yale School of Forestry & Environmental Studies. (2010). Do Americans' actions speak louder than words on climate and energy? *Yale Project on Climate Change Communication*. Retrieved from: http://environment.yale.edu/climate-communication/article/do-americans-actions-speak-louder-than-words-on-climate-energy/

Zubizarreta, J. (2009). *The learning portfolio: Reflective practice for improving student learning (2nd Ed.)*. San Francisco: Jossey-Bass.

Index

....

The letter *f* following a page number denotes a figure.

About the Authors

Pete Hall

Veteran school administrator and professional development agent Pete Hall has dedicated his career to supporting the improvement of our education systems. Besides partnering with Alisa Simeral on this and their first book together, he authored *The First-Year Principal* (Scarecrow Education, 2004) and *Lead On! Motivational Lessons for School Leaders* (Eye on Education, 2011). Pete currently works as an educational consultant as a member of the ASCD faculty and trains educators worldwide. You can contact him via e-mail at Pete.Hall.Faculty@ASCD.org or catch his Twitter feeds at @EducationHall.

Alisa Simeral

School turnaround specialist and veteran educator Alisa Simeral has guided school-based reform efforts as a teacher, dean, and instructional coach. Her emphasis is, and always has been, improving the adult-input factors that contribute to the betterment of the student-output results. She partnered with Pete Hall to write their first book together, *Building Teachers' Capacity for Success: A Collaborative Approach for Coaches and School Leaders* (ASCD, 2008), and already has plans for their next writing venture. Passionate about providing support where it's needed most—at the classroom level—her mantra is "When our teachers succeed, our students succeed."